RETURN
PATAGON

BY WAY OF THE FALKLAND ISLANDS

RETURN to PATAGONIA

BY WAY OF THE FALKLAND ISLANDS

ROSEMARY J. GORING

Peter Owen
London and Chester Springs

ISBN 0 7206 1260 8

PETER OWEN PUBLISHERS
73 Kenway Road, London SW5 0RE

Peter Owen books are distributed in the USA by
Dufour Editions Inc., Chester Springs, PA 19425-0007

First published 2006
© Rosemary J. Goring 2006

Printed and bound in Great Britain by
Windsor Print Production Ltd, Tonbridge, Kent

In memory of my parents

ACKNOWLEDGEMENTS

I owe a special debt of gratitude to my cousin Mary Trehearne for allowing me to quote freely from her books *Falkland Heritage* and *Patagonian Harvest*, which have provided open access to a great deal of original material. Thanks are due to Angela Wigglesworth for permission to quote from her book *Falkland People* and to John Pilkington for passages from his book *An Englishman in Patagonia*. I am grateful also to Graham Bound and to John Smith for allowing me to quote from *Falkland Islanders at War* and *74 Days* respectively. Roedean archivist Jackie Sullivan was extremely helpful in providing material about my mother.

Many thanks to my brother Hugh, who regrettably did not live to see the book in print, for his painstaking work on the maps and family trees and for helpful comments on the manuscript. Thanks, too, to my brother John for further corrections and clarifications and permission to quote from some pieces of writing, to my sister Eleanor Dixon for words of encouragement and to everyone at Peter Owen Publishers for their friendliness and efficiency. Most of all I am grateful to my husband Jeremy for his unfailing support and advice – and to my nephew Stuart for those airline tickets without which the journey to Patagonia could never have taken place.

We are greatly indebted to John and Monica for making their flat available to us in Buenos Aires and for their kind hospitality at Killik Aike Norte. Our thanks go, too, to Lilián Burlando for looking after us so well in Ushuaia. And something I shall never forget is the welcome that we received from Cath Mann and Lidia Pickering in San Julián.

AUTHOR'S PREFACE

Like the two journeys described in this book, my decision to write *Return to Patagonia* was not a matter of advance planning. What happened was that, at the conclusion of the trip that my husband and I took to Patagonia, I decided to transcribe the travel journal I had kept throughout and make it into a small booklet to be circulated among family and friends.

But at this point technology intervened. I was nine-tenths of the way through the transcription when my machine – at that time not a computer but an enhanced electronic typewriter – flashed up the message: MEMORY FULL. In attempting to deal with the problem I hit the wrong button and lost the lot. Rather than go back and start all over again, I took it as an indication that I should do something different. Why not expand the whole project and turn it into a book? Why not also add in the account of the visit to the Falkland Islands that I had made seven years before?

I already knew that the book my brother was then writing included a great deal about the general history of the British in southern Patagonia. What I was seeking to do, however, was something different: to tell the story of a personal pilgrimage, with historical background filled in where necessary. At the same time I realized that, having close family connections on both sides of the water, I was perhaps in the unique position of being able to describe, for the benefit of both parties in the South Atlantic conflict, something of what it felt like to be in the other person's shoes.

Travel-book connoisseurs will be aware that – by chance rather than design – the Patagonian part of my journey follows what has become known as the 'Chatwin Trail'. The famous writer passed rapidly through the landscape, collecting characters as he went. The Patagonia familiar to me from my childhood, with which I was once again able to make contact, represents a different sort of experience. This book is mainly about the rediscovery of a network of relationships extending across the region and down the years. The place is surely big enough for both kinds of writer.

Rosemary J. Goring
2006

CONTENTS

1 LEAVING CORONEL 13

2 EAST FALKLAND 21

3 WEST FALKLAND 33

4 BUENOS AIRES 43

5 TRELEW 53

6 COMODORO 63

7 SAN JULIÁN: BEGINNINGS 73

8 EARLY DAYS AT CORONEL 81

9 IN SAN JULIÁN 91

10 BACK TO CORONEL 103

11 RÍO GALLEGOS 115

12 TIERRA DEL FUEGO 125

13 KILLIK AIKE 137

14 CENTENARY 149

Chronological Tables of Argentina
and the Falkland Islands 161

Family Trees of the Blake and Mann Families 165

Bibliography 167

Index 169

Illustrations and maps between pages 96 and 97

Patagonia

Line upon endless line of barren hills,
Brown, barren, flat-topped hills, fading away
Into immense purple distances
Beyond the bleak horizon. A windmill stands,
Stark skeleton, against the hard sapphire sky.

And wind: the never-ceasing, hard, dry wind,
Whistling through stiff, bristly tussocks of stinging grass,
Quivering the gnarled, crabby-fingered bushes,
Whipping up eddies of dust which spinningly stagger
Down the valley. Out of the wind-battered silence
Spirals the thin, solitary 'baa'
Of a single sheep, lonely in the vast wilderness . . .

The peewits' piercing panic-stricken cries
Burst from the ground with the black-white liveried birds,
And a hare breaks cover close by, racing hard,
Ears flat, up the black-bush-dotted slope.

A pale brown ribbon, linking hills together –
The track: and on it, one black beetle crawling –
A car, dwarfed by the hills' encircling hugeness –
Startles a herd of guanaco, poised on the skyline,
Who lollop lazily off, sailing easily over
The fence, thin line that straggles on forever.

Smooth round sea-worn pebbles, scant dry grass,
A threadbare garment for the arid earth:
An endless, empty land, dry desolation . . .

But lo! in the valley, a thick green carpet spread,
And trees, willows and poplars, gracefully bending,
Red roofs, and running water, sweet spring water,
And Eden blooming in the wilderness!

Rosemary J. Goring (née Blake), October 1951

1. Leaving Coronel

After supper, the evening before we were due to leave the farm, I slipped out of the house, leaving the other two at their game of table tennis. It was early March; autumn had not yet arrived. I climbed the shallow side of the valley until I reached a small spur from which I could see the whole of the main settlement of Estancia Coronel spread out below me.

Up the valley to my left lay the red roof of the Casa Grande, the Big House where we lived, surrounded by its trees and its gardens, looking out over the concrete tennis court. On the other side of this stood the tall clump of willows beside the little stream that ran down the centre of the valley. Very green the trees appeared against the dun-coloured slope of the Stony Hill on the opposite side, worn bare over the years by the small hooves of thousands of sheep. A little further down the valley were the single-storey dwellings of the other families who lived on the farm, each with its own small garden. Below me to my right stood the cook-house and shepherds' quarters together with the store, the butcher's and the carpenter's workshop; beyond them lay the dog-kennels and pigsties, the sturdy wooden posts of the horse-corral and the maze of sheep corrals abutting the long line of the shearing-shed. Just visible in front of this was the long narrow trough of the sheep-dip. Further away, in No. 5 paddock, could be seen the pedigree rams' shed, with the old wooden *chata* – the great horse-drawn wagon that used to trundle the wool bales down to the coast in days gone by – standing marooned in its own patch of green. And beyond this loomed the distinctive conical shape of Cerro Munro, named after the shepherd who had first come over from the Falkland Islands in 1891 to settle in this uninhabited valley.

This was the main settlement – but further afield, I knew, dispersed across the farm's 550 square miles of bare, open, windswept land, were the subsidiary settlements: New Dip, Ferreiri, Cabo Curioso and the shepherds' shanties at Square Hill and Cañadón Sam.

There lay the settlement in the evening light, just as I had always known it throughout the eleven years of my childhood. At that point the truth hit me. For weeks now our parents had been going off to attend *despedidas*, farewell parties hosted by all the friends and neighbours with whom they had shared so many years of their lives. But now the time had run out. Tomorrow we were going 'home' to England, and I was never going to see the place again. I had come up here, I now realized, in order to say goodbye. I went down on my knees on that stony, prickly ground and wept.

'Where have you been?' they asked as I came back into the house.

'Just for a walk,' I said.

The following day, which was 12 March 1947, we drove down to the port of San Julián and, in a final flurry of farewells, embarked on the passenger ship *Asturiano* for the ten-day voyage up the coast to Buenos Aires.

One connection with the farm still remained. Agnes, who had been our playmate there for many years, was travelling with us as far as the Welsh town of Trelew to start her next term at St David's, the English-speaking school that provided an education for a number of the British children in Patagonia. We said goodbye to each other when the *Asturiano* put in at Puerto Madryn, promising to write. But somehow we never did.

Our leisurely boat trip up the coast of Patagonia was followed by more waiting in Buenos Aires, for travel to Europe was still in a state of post-war flux. Eventually my mother, sister Eleanor and I were able to get seats on a British South American Airways flight. It was a converted Lancaster bomber and very noisy. My father and brother Hugh, travelling with the heavy luggage, considered themselves lucky to get two passages on a cargo boat travelling via the Canaries. Our eldest brother John, who was following our father into the sheep-farming business, had already left Argentina and was learning the first-hand practicalities on the other family farm in the Falkland Islands.

It was 17 April when we landed at Heathrow. Seven years and a world war separated us from our last time in England, and I looked around me in amazement. It seemed slightly comical, I don't know why, to see everything written up in English. I was only five when last in England, and for all of my literate life had been surrounded by public notices in Spanish.

A porter came up to us, his words sounding strange in my ears. 'Can I carry your bag, missy?'

We were 'home'.

The tall figure of our grandmother – alone, for our mother's father, Philip Worsley, had died in 1945 – was waiting for us at Temple Meads Station. As we drove through Bristol the weed-covered open spaces and ruined buildings of the bomb sites told their own story of what the city had been through during the war. Half an hour's drive through a West Country landscape of green hills and ploughed fields of rich red Somerset earth brought us to Westfield in the village of Winscombe, where not a great deal seemed to have changed since we were last there in 1940. This large, pleasant house, with a generous garden and superb view of the Mendip hills, was now to be our home.

'You're as brown as berries!' people said to my sister and me. For we had come straight from summer, while post-war Britain was still struggling to recover from an exceptionally hard winter, complete with fuel shortages and power cuts. We had to go to the neighbouring town of Axbridge to collect our ration books. One of the first things I did was to spill the entire week's sugar ration – which didn't amount to very much – all over the brown linoleum of the kitchen floor. Frantic efforts were made to retrieve as much of it as was hygienically possible. This was a far cry from the large wooden tub standing in the larder of the Casa Grande which was never empty and from which I could pick out a lump or two whenever I felt inclined.

The next thing – for my sister Eleanor and me at least – was getting ready for boarding-school. This was nothing new, for we had been at boarding-school in Buenos Aires – St Hilda's – since the ages of nine and ten. Now we were to go to our mother and grandmother's old school, Roedean, perched high on the Sussex cliff-top near Brighton. They had both been happy there, so we supposed we should be, too. It was then only two years since the school had returned to its own buildings after being evacuated to Keswick in the Lake District. This had evidently been quite an adventure, and those of us who had not been there sometimes felt as if we had missed out on something rather special. There was, however, one huge bonus as far as Eleanor and I were concerned.

The school year in Argentina was made up of two long terms. The winter holiday was only a matter of two to three weeks, and the distance was too great and the weather too uncertain to make the trip home to Patagonia worth our while. Our parents would fly up to join us in Buenos Aires, our brothers would come across the Andes from their school – the Grange – in Santiago, and we would spend the time, in the company of other British families, at a pleasant holiday hotel, formerly an old monastery, near Villa Dolores in the province of Córdoba, in the foothills of the Andes. We only went home once a year for the summer holidays in December, which lasted for three full months. But here in England we were able to get home three times in the year, and to us this seemed a great luxury.

Our first summer in England was fine, warm and dry. My father and Hugh had now arrived, and we heard the story of how their cargo boat, leaving the Canaries with a load of tomatoes, struck a storm and had the fruit rolling all over the deck. The family group was finally completed by John's arrival from the Falklands. In August we enjoyed a traditional seaside holiday in Wales with uncles, aunts and a raft of cousins. There was a lot of family to catch up on. Everyone was glad to see us back.

'Home at last!' they said. 'Aren't you pleased to be home?'

For the first time in years we celebrated Christmas in the middle of winter. There was holly, ivy and mistletoe to decorate the house, and it was in every way a typical traditional English country Christmas. How strange to think that this time last year we were having an *asado*, the traditional whole-sheep barbecue, out in the blazing sun! It all seemed so far away, in time as well as in distance.

So, little by little, we became reintegrated into the British way of life, and new impressions, one by one, overlaid the experiences of earlier years. From time to time recollections would surface to find expression in stories or poems such as the one I wrote in 1951 at the age of sixteen, four years after our departure. Our parents continued to maintain the link with Argentina; my father travelled out every year between 1948 and 1970 to keep an eye on the affairs of the farm, and sometimes my mother would go with him. In this way we continued to be linked to the people we had grown up with. Our lives ran in parallel, the gulf between the two hemispheres bridged by the reassuring figures of our parents.

One by one we completed our education, embarked on careers, found partners, married, had children of our own. Our parents, and our elder brother John with his growing family, continued to embody the Argentine experience while we, the remaining three, got on with our individual lives from an English base. But by now John had become the manager of Condor, another much bigger farm further south belonging to a different company, so that the link with our own family farm was now virtually dependent on just two people, who were not getting any younger.

In 1964 came the sudden death of our mother at the untimely age of sixty-three. Our father made a few trips out to Patagonia on his own until a stroke put an end to any further prospect of long-distance travel. Meanwhile, changing conditions in both Britain and Argentina were obliging the San Julián Sheep Farming Company's board of directors to rethink their management strategy. This resulted in the liquidation of the British company in 1973 and its replacement by the Argentine 'Ganadera Coronel'. By the time of my father's death in 1976 it was clear that the company was struggling, and in 1978 one of the directors made an offer for the farm that the others were glad to accept. This was how the farm that had been our childhood home eventually passed into someone else's hands.

Some time in the 1980s I had a dream about Coronel. I was standing in the middle of the settlement, just by the little stream that trickled down the middle of the valley. Night had fallen. I crossed over the bridge, or rather the walkway of planks that led from one side to the other, and made my way down to the shearing shed. Lights were on inside, and I went in to explore. Men were at work repairing the building – and they were talking to one another, I noticed, not in Spanish but Italian. I walked through the shed and out the other end, continuing along the track that led down the valley away from the farm. Then I saw in the darkness something quite unexpected. It was a procession of alligators – creatures quite alien to Patagonia – crossing the track from left to right, the moonlight glinting on their black-and-green scaly backs. There were an awful lot of them, and although they ignored me completely they seemed dangerous. So I turned back – and then woke up.

My childhood, meanwhile, remained locked away in the Southern Hemisphere.

In the autumn of 1981 my brother and sister-in-law came over for a visit. John's career in sheep farming had taken off in a big way. In addition to being the manager of Condor, a farm the size of an English county and shearing 110,000 sheep, he had also been able to purchase another smaller farm on the coast near Río Gallegos. It was called Killik Aike Norte and was to be his family home when the time came for him to retire. This trip to Britain was rather a special one involving a visit to Buckingham Palace, because John had recently been awarded the OBE for services to the British community in Argentina.

Our second son George happened to be at home; he had left school the previous year and was uncertain what to do next.

'Why not spend a few months with us at Condor?' John suggested. 'We're always glad of more hands at shearing time and, you never know, you might develop a taste for the life.'

It was not until later that we heard about some of the problems that had surfaced in Argentina while John and Monica were admiring the décor of Buckingham Palace. During their absence Killik Aike had been taken over by the army for training purposes. So what exactly was the Argentine army doing, practising landing manoeuvres on the coast of the South Atlantic? The exercises were under the supervision of the commander-in-chief of the Fifth Army Division, which covered all of Patagonia: General Leopoldo Galtieri.

John's third son Stuart was just doing his military service in the Coast Guard at Río Gallegos at the time, and on one of his visits to Killik Aike he found himself serving *maté* (the local tea) to the General. As an extremely junior recruit, he found it somewhat awkward to point out to the General that, if his tanks stopped and opened gates rather than drove through them, then that year's breeding programme would not be thrown into disarray. In addition, he had to fend off enquiries as to the availability of accommodation in the Casa Grande; all this while explaining that the owner, was, at the time, in the UK being received by the Queen.

My brother, on his return to the farm, was astonished to discover how much damage had been done, both to stock and to fencing, in so short a time – but he never received a single peso in compensation. Meanwhile, on 22 December, General Galtieri moved into much more congenial accommodation: the Casa Rosada, traditional residence of the Presidents of Argentina.

George, together with his cousin Piers Worsley, who had also decided to sample life in Patagonia, eventually left for Argentina in January 1982 – by which time, as it happened, the shearing season was nearly over. Letters to us arrived regularly, awakening familiar memories of life on a big sheep farm. Towards the end of George's three months' stay he began to talk about moving on to other parts of Argentina. He might, for example, spend some time with the Wood cousins whose farm, Huechahue, was in the province of Neuquén, the beautiful western lake district overshadowed by the Andes.

'Or what about', I suggested in a letter, 'seeing if you can get over to the Falklands to visit the Blake cousins there?' George's reply arrived at the end of March, saying that he had written to Tim and Sally, the cousins in question, suggesting a visit to Hill Cove in West Falkland. Then, on 2 April, Argentina invaded the Falkland Islands.

We had absolutely no idea where George was. If he had left Condor, which way had he gone, north to Neuquén – or across the sea to the Falklands? It was ten days before his airmail letter arrived telling us that he had done neither. He had gone south and was currently hitch-hiking in Tierra del Fuego. While we had been hanging on the words of every available news bulletin, he had been camping out under Antarctic beeches in the peace of the Lapataia National Park. We later heard that John had put George's letter addressed to the Falkland Islands in his pocket but decided not to send it. When news of the Argentine invasion came through it was clear that both George and Piers, whose temporary visitors' visas had almost expired, should leave the country as soon as possible. He advised George, on his return from his camping trip, to head south once more, so that he would be able to make his way home without having to travel through Argentina.

Uninterrupted travel, however, could no longer be taken for granted. As George's long-distance coach in Gallegos was about to depart, uniformed soldiers climbed on board and took him and a number of other passengers away for questioning, and the coach left for Punta Arenas without them. A courteous, white-haired officer enquired why he wished to leave Argentina. George explained that his tourist visa had expired and added, 'The relations between our two countries are not too good at the moment.'

'There are no problems between our two countries,' declared the officer. For the British Task Force had not yet set sail and, as far as Argentina was concerned, everything was fine.

When he was finally able to resume his journey, George had no difficulty in crossing the border and heading north from the Chilean port of Punta Arenas. Travelling through Chile was a much more relaxing experience. The two countries had for years been at loggerheads over certain islands in the Beagle Channel – which cuts through Tierra del Fuego more or less parallel with the Magellan Straits – and so Chile was a natural supporter of anyone who was against Argentina. George's British nationality made him instantly popular, and he had a pleasant journey up the western coast of Chilean Patagonia until he reached Santiago, from where he was able to book a flight back to Britain via Río de Janeiro. We were mightily glad to welcome him home. Cousin Piers, too, eventually returned to England and opted for a different career altogether.

2. EAST FALKLAND

The Falklands conflict was by this time at its height, and our stance was unashamedly pro-British. We drove around our Sussex village and all the country lanes with *Keep Falkland Islands British* plastered across our rear window – and discovered that other friends in the neighbourhood also had Falkland connections.

'My mother was a Bertrand,' said someone in the village; another was related to the Feltons. A third, Gwerfyl Brooks, turned out to be descended from one of the nineteenth-century governors of the Falklands, Colonel George D'Arcy, whose term of office, we found, coincided with the time that my grandfather Robert Blake arrived there as a young man in 1873. She and I spent a pleasant evening together sharing information about these remote and little-known islands, with a population of only 2,000, which had been so suddenly projected into the national consciousness.

When the Islands were finally recaptured on 14 June 1982 my husband Jeremy and I attended the modest victory celebrations up in London. We were relieved to hear that Tim and Sally Blake on West Falkland had had a relatively quiet war: a single Argentine pilot shot down, whom they looked after in their own home, and a contingent of Black Watch billeted on the farm after hostilities had ended.

After this came the collapse of the military regime in Argentina and the establishment of civilian rule. The rest of the world watched with interest and some sympathy as the country began the difficult process of coming to terms with the horrendous human rights abuses of the previous six years. Meanwhile, in both Britain and Argentina, the question of Falklands sovereignty continued to be a political hot potato.

The Falkland Islanders themselves had very definite views on the matter. In August 1988 two members of the Falkland Islands Legislative Council, Robin Lee and Tim Blake, went to the United Nations in New York to speak to a resolution tabled by Argentina. My cousin concluded his speech with these words:

It is our mission here to point out that the future of the Falkland Islands is for us the Falkland Islanders to decide. We do not wish to become either a part of Great Britain or of Argentina . . . It should be recognized we made the Islands what they are today, and we would wish that they should be under our control with the government of our choice. It would seem to me that the resolution before the Committee seeks in no way to give us such freedom but to make us more dependent on a different government.

The United Nations duly took note of the wishes of the Islanders and did not rule in favour of Argentina. Britain nevertheless continued to maintain a strong military presence in the Islands – just in case.

I remained a member of the Falkland Islands Association for some years after the conflict, and in August 1991 an eye-catching advertisement appeared in the *Newsletter*:

> The Reverend Peter Millam and Major Ronnie Spafford invite you to
> come with them
> on the unique visit for Pilgrims and Philatelists to the
> FALKLAND ISLANDS
> For the 100th Anniversary of the Consecration
> of Christ Church Cathedral
> February 17 to March 1, 1992

George Carey, the newly appointed Archbishop of Canterbury, would attend the centenary service, and there were also going to be visits to some of the spectacular wildlife sites for which the Islands are famous. What was unsaid – but in everyone's minds – was that it would be the tenth anniversary of the war.

What an opportunity! I thought. There might be a chance to visit Hill Cove, the farm where my father had been born, and to fill in this part of the background to our family story. I would be able to meet up again with Tim, my contemporary whom I had not seen for many years, and his Falklands-born wife Sally. The offer was certainly a tempting one. But it would cost too much for both Jeremy and myself to go, and I did not fancy travelling on my own. Then came a phone call from our old friend Gwerfyl Brooks.

'Have you seen the advert in the *Newsletter*? The children think I should go, but it would be nice to have a travelling companion. Do give it serious thought – I feel it is a chance not to be missed.'

And so Gwerfyl and I wrote off for information and booked our places on the tour.

Gwerfyl's son-in-law, Rick from New Zealand, drove us to RAF Brize Norton on the evening of 17 February 1992. There were security checks at the gates and none of the tourist-friendly trappings of a civilian airport. One by one the other members of the party assembled, fifteen of us in all; it was the largest-ever tour by air to the Falklands. Our TriStar jet, acquired second-hand from Pan Am, eventually took off at midnight.

About three o'clock the following afternoon I was astonished to look out of my porthole and see a dark, sinister-looking fighter plane flying alongside. It was a Phantom jet, escorting us in to our landing at the military airport of Mount Pleasant. As we stepped out on to the tarmac that represented our first encounter with Falklands soil, jets were roaring overhead and the military presence was heavily in evidence. Costing £70 million a year and housing anything up to 2,000 military personnel, this base, with its fighter aircraft, helicopters, naval patrol craft, radar and anti-aircraft missile systems, was making quite sure that there were to be no more Argentine military adventures.

So I was not altogether surprised when, as we passed through customs, I alone of all the party was asked to open my suitcase, which was searched politely but thoroughly. After all, my place of birth was there on my passport for all to see: *Buenos Aires, Argentina*. The precaution was understandable in view of the next part of the proceedings, which consisted of a briefing about mines and other unexploded missiles which, ten years after the war had ended, still presented a very real threat. Indeed, even twenty years after the conflict between 25,000 and 30,000 mines were still to be found in 117 locations all over the Islands.

It was something of a relief, after all this, to climb into a homely-looking coach for the hour-long ride into Stanley. It did not seem that much had changed since Charles Darwin visited the Islands in the *Beagle* in 1833 and 1834:

An undulating land, with a desolate and wretched aspect, is every where covered by a peaty soil and wiry grass, of one monotonous brown colour. Here and there a peak or ridge of grey quartz rock breaks through the smooth surface . . .

To me the uninhabited, treeless landscape, bleak as it was, had a certain reassuring familiarity, recalling the windswept Patagonia that I remembered from my childhood. But what were the things that looked like wide grey glaciers flowing down some of the hills? These were the mysterious 'stone runs' for which, we were told, no geological explanation had yet been found.

Port Stanley, when we got there, was another surprise: so small, so neat, so homely. But after our long, exhausting journey it provided exactly the kind of informal, friendly welcome we needed. I was pleased to discover that our half of the party were lodged in the Upland Goose Hotel, for I knew that my parents had stayed there when visiting in the 1950s.

As soon as I could, I rang my cousins on West Falkland. I knew that the tour would be taking us to Port Howard, one of the other farms on that island, and I wondered whether it might be possible for me to make some sort of a detour and call in on the old family farm.

'At any other time of the year,' said Tim, 'there would be no problem. But it's Sports Week. Last year everyone came to Hill Cove but this year it's Port Howard's turn, so we shall all be going over there.'

Just my luck! I knew enough about Falklands life to understand what Sports Week meant. It takes place when everyone has finished shearing and is an opportunity for people to get together, celebrate and relax. On West Falkland the larger farms take it in turns to be host to the visitors from all the other farms on the island. Everyone beds down on the floor in impromptu dormitories; there is plenty to eat and, above all, to drink. Entertainment is home grown: there are races and competitions and dancing to music provided by local talent. I do not think anyone gets much sleep.

What all this meant for me was that, while I would certainly be able to meet up with Tim and Sally – since they would be coming into Stanley for the centenary service at the cathedral – a visit to Hill Cove was really out of the question. For, instead of travelling together as a single tour unit, the Pilgrims and Philatelists were to be in two groups, each with a separate itinerary, and I did not want to add to the existing complications.

When our group arrived at Stanley Airport next morning and saw the transport provided by the Falkland Islands Government Air Service – FIGAS for short – we understood the reason for this arrangement. The bright red Islander airplanes seated exactly ten people, including the pilot, which meant that only eight tour members at a time could travel to any given destination. Today the others were flying to Sea Lion Island, while our group was bound for Goose Green.

It was a marvellous travel experience. The cruising height of such a small aircraft was low enough for us to be able to take in every detail on the grey-green surface of the island: every inlet along the coast, every is.. farmstead, with sheep scattered around like grains of rice. We followed . line of the road being newly extended from Mount Pleasant to Darwin, the only proper road on the Islands. Apart from Stanley and its environs, Falklanders were used to bumping over rough farm tracks or simply taking off across country, for the way to get easily from one part of the Islands to another had always been either by ship or, latterly, by air. Otherwise, before the days of the Land-Rover, it was simply a question of horseback.

'This is the Goose Green airstrip,' we were told as the airplane touched down on a bare, windy stretch of grassland, the only sign of life consisting of two Land-Rovers standing next to a small corrugated-iron hut. We headed down to Darwin farm settlement and the travel lodge, formerly the manager's house. The late summer sun was warm on our backs. Groups of birds, some white and some rust-coloured, wandered over the grass between the buildings, as tame as farmyard fowl: the ever-present upland geese.

An hour later, full of coffee and home-made cake, we were ready to begin exploring. A short journey of about half a mile took us up on to a bare open hillside, and there ahead of us lay a large square piece of land with white wooden fencing all round it, enclosing rows and rows of small white crosses, 235 in all. It was the Argentine war cemetery.

Nobody had much to say as we strolled round the neatly kept paths, accompanied only by the sound of the incessant wind. The open, empty landscape fell away around us, leading to glimpses of blue sea, with further headlands beyond. Anyone who hailed from the Western Isles of Scotland would feel at home here, I thought. It was impossible to imagine a battle raging in such a peaceful place. Yet a little way downhill we came on a small whitewashed rectangle set in the upland turf, marking the spot where Colonel 'H' Jones of 2 Parachute Battalion had fallen in the attack to retake Goose Green. A little further on the Land-Rover suddenly stopped for no apparent reason. Then as we got out and looked around we saw a patch of ground beside the track, looking no different from anywhere else except that it was roughly enclosed by a single strand of wire. A red notice displaying a skull and crossbones warned: DANGER – MINES. The deadly canisters of napalm that had been stored at Goose Green under the Argentine occupation had long been removed, but the mines remained as a lasting legacy. Children now knew as a matter of course that if by chance a ball got thrown into one of these enclosures you just left it there and never tried to get it back.

Goose Green ten years later showed no signs of any sort of conflict, other than a simple cross commemorating the seventeen British

ho had fallen in the battle. Arriving in the middle of the
-painted, red-roofed buildings, we involuntarily sniffed the
ered out of our vehicles. What was this tangy, musky, all-
The answer lay straight ahead of us. Behind every house
wooden pen piled high with rich dark-brown squares of peat, the
islands' only fuel. It had none of the sweet, woody fragrance familiar to
dwellers in Scotland, Ireland or the Somerset moors because it was made
up of a completely different set of plants – but it was clearly the same
article. As we looked around, the community hall where 115 islanders had
been confined during the conflict was immediately identifiable. We had a
chat with one of the local inhabitants and called in at the Goose Green
Stores.

Our tour had not come, however, simply to rake over the ashes of the past.
Many in the group had a particular interest in the other, non-human
inhabitants of the Islands, and down by the shore we watched a group of
them contentedly paddling in and out of the water: the kelp geese, the
ruddy-headed geese, the upland geese, the flightless steamer ducks. A little
further on we peered through the rotting timbers of a long-abandoned ship
called the *Vicar of Bray* to see the outline of a nesting night heron.

'You'll be seeing plenty of wildlife tomorrow,' we were promised, 'when
we get to Sea Lion Island.'

Our base on Sea Lion Island was a modern, purpose-built tourist hostel
looking out over an expanse of land covered with red sheep's sorrel. Beyond
this, although we could not see it, was the beach. The flat, reddish-coloured
terrain was pocked with small burrows housing the small Magellanic or
jackass penguins, one of the five varieties of penguin to be found on the
islands. They popped up to look at us as we went past, and we lost our hearts
to them immediately.

During the course of the day we walked through a large colony of gentoo
penguins, stepped over the huge basking bodies of elephant seal, spotted
several unfamiliar varieties of teal and widgeon, scanned from a safe distance
the activities of a colony of southern sea lion and clambered through a
rookery of black-and-white king cormorants and rockhopper penguins.
None of these creatures took the slightest notice of our intrusion. Perhaps
the strongest impression that remained with me from seeing so many
different species getting on with their lives in their normal way was that
there did not seem to be all that much difference between their social
organization and that of human beings.

There was another sight to be seen on Sea Lion Island, but this one was inanimate and man-made. It was a memorial to HMS *Sheffield*, the first casualty of the war, sunk by an Argentine Exocet while cruising these remote southern waters.

The next three nights were spent in Stanley. In unusually sunny and windless weather we went on a boat trip round the harbour. Lining the waterfront was a succession of ancient ships in varying stages of decrepitude, and we learnt that Stanley was a maritime museum in its own right – one indeed of worldwide importance. Accompanied, to our delight, by a couple of porpoises, we cut across to Port William on the other side of the bay, as far as Sparrow Cove. This for many years had been the resting-place of Brunel's *Great Britain* – the first iron ship in the world – until she was brought back to England and installed in her home port of Bristol. As our motor launch swung round for the return journey we were able to look astern at the western end of the bay and see the sharp triangular peaks of Mount Tumbledown with Mount Harriet and the Two Sisters just beyond – the setting for the final British assault on Stanley in June 1982.

We had just time, once back on dry land, to smarten ourselves up and comb our wind-blown hair before our next appointment: tea at Government House with the Governor, William Fullerton, and his American wife Arlene. They made us feel quite at home as we sat in the elegant drawing-room balancing cups of tea on our knees and demolishing platefuls of home-made scones and cake. Gwerfyl was introduced as a descendant of a previous governor, and my family credentials were brought to the fore. After tea we were given a tour of Government House, including a visit to the Governor's office. Here we were able to see the desk under which one of Sir William's predecessors, Sir Rex Hunt, had been obliged to shelter in the early hours of 2 April 1982 while Argentine soldiers were besieging Government House.

The following day we headed out of town in a convoy of Land-Rovers, bound for the north-eastern part of the island. It was an hour's run to Port Louis, providing plenty of time for conversation with our driver, a young man by the name of Tony Smith.

'What did people in the islands feel like,' we asked him, 'during the years before the Argentine invasion?' Tony was able to convey very effectively the feeling of unease that was prevalent in the islands at that time, when the

British government seemed to be conducting a series of deals with Argentina over the heads of the islanders themselves. At the same time, disquieting information was starting to leak out via Amnesty International about the human rights abuses committed by the Argentine military regime. This made the islanders feel very nervous. They all knew what the endgame was – annexation to Argentina – but there was nothing they could do about it. They were being stalked, and they knew it.

At last we arrived at Port Louis, the historic first settlement on the islands, on the shores of Berkeley Sound. The site dated from 1764, and the outlines of the original French fort and cemetery could still be discerned. The road, or rather track, ended here – and so did the opportunity for further conversation. For the next two hours we were travelling cross-country over uninhabited terrain, bumping over tussocks of turf, swerving round the heads of watercourses, lurching down into little gullies and up the opposite side, somehow managing not to end up in the middle of a bog. The skill of our drivers – a typically Falklands accomplishment – was phenomenal. We discovered that being a passenger required some skill as well.

We took a welcome break at Johnson's Harbour settlement, where some of the local residents came up for a chat. I was introduced as Tim Blake's cousin.

'Yes,' they said, considering me thoughtfully, 'you look like a Blake.'

At midday we reached Volunteer Point and parked in a small ravine. As we clambered up the shallow slope towards higher ground a sound caught our ears. Was it singing? A little further on we could see where the music was coming from: a large group of figures was standing in a dense circle, their heads raised in a wordless chant. Here was the king penguin colony we had come so far to see.

The handsome birds, about half the height of a human being, did not share the black-and-white colour scheme of their smaller relations. They had the same white shirt-fronts, but their backs were a steely grey, and their black heads and necks were enlivened by splashes of vivid orange. They held their slender heads high and walked with a dignified air, taking our camera-crazy group perfectly in their stride. We all agreed, as we bumped our way back to Stanley, that the experience had been worth the bone-shaking.

In the early evening it was time to experience an assembly of human beings. The Archbishop of Canterbury was now in town, and we were invited to attend the reception at the Assembly Rooms held in his honour. It was not difficult to spot my cousin Tim, for although we had not met for years he bore a striking resemblance to his father, my Uncle Norman.

The youngest of the Blake family of eight, Norman had been born in the

Falklands and was the third son of that generation to go into farming. But while his two elder brothers, Robert and my father Arthur, had both been involved in the development of the farm in Patagonia, Norman settled near the family home in Somerset. Here he developed his radical ideas on raising free-range pigs, setting out his findings in a small book, published by Faber and Faber in 1956, called *The Pioneering Pig*. Tim therefore grew up in England, and his only experience of Argentina was the time he spent at Condor learning the ins and outs of sheep farming under the tutelage of my brother John. The youngest son of the youngest son, he was now farming on the original site where his grandfather had arrived as a young man in 1873.

Sally, Tim's wife, greeted me warmly. A Kelper born and bred, she was descended from the Bertrands of Roy Cove, another of the original farming families on West Falkland.

'Come and have supper with us,' they said. It was only a few minutes' walk to the comfortable house that was their base in Stanley, and soon we were catching up on family affairs.

A good deal of our talk focused on the changes that had taken place in sheep farming during the ten years since 1982. The old company system of farming, run by managers answerable to shareholders and a board of directors in England, had evidently been ripe for change. Kindly and paternalistic though it was, the age of the absentee owner was at an end. Employees in the islands now wanted more independence and responsibility in the running of the farms. One by one the large landholdings had been sold to the Falkland Islands Development Corporation which was then able to divide up the land and resell it to those wishing to run smaller, independent farms. Preferential treatment was given to former employees. Hill Cove was sold in 1987 and divided into eight sections. Tim was now looking after 7,000 sheep, as opposed to the 34,000 he had been dealing with when he was manager of the original company of Holmested Blake. It felt very strange at first, he confessed. But they had enjoyed setting up The Peaks – one of the smaller sections – and farming it and were still living in the same house at Hill Cove that had been built by our grandfather in 1882 – the house I would not be able to visit. Their two sons, Paul and Alex, were looking at different career opportunities, which might or might not be based in the Falklands. They were not bound to follow their father into sheep farming.

'See you at the cathedral tomorrow,' we said to one another at the end of the evening, for Sally would be reading one of the lessons at the centenary service. Stanley on a Saturday night seemed remarkably quiet; there was hardly anyone to be seen on the short stroll along the waterfront to the welcoming lights of the Upland Goose.

Christ Church Cathedral, first consecrated in February 1892, was a solid, red-brick structure about the size of a large parish church, with only two features that distinguished it from any number of ecclesiastical buildings of the same period to be found in the British Isles. One was the white, curiously shaped double arch set within the small cathedral precinct, formed from the huge jawbones of a blue whale. The other was the extraordinary show of colour in the flower beds lining the approach to the cathedral. Not only were there the usual late summer blooms appropriate to the time of year but also a great array of daffodils whose bulbs were still attuned to the biorhythms of the northern hemisphere.

Every seat was taken for the ten o'clock service, and a round of applause greeted the Archbishop of Canterbury, Dr George Carey, as the procession of clergy came up the aisle. This was the first time an archbishop had come to the islands, but there was a particular reason for the visit: the cathedral since 1982 had been placed under his personal jurisdiction. Other dignitaries included Colin Bazeley, Presiding Bishop of the Anglican Church of the Southern Cone of America, and Monsignor Anton Agreiter, who was now in charge of the Catholic Church in Stanley. This little church, under Monsignor Daniel Spraggon, had played a pivotal role during the time of the occupation. It provided essential communication with Argentine officialdom, who were obliged to respect its authority, and also much-needed spiritual comfort for the unhappy, frightened young Argentine conscripts.

Dr Carey, during the course of his address, made the point that, although many who bore scars of the war still found it difficult to forgive or forget, Christians should look beyond human limitations to seek reconciliation with those who had harmed them. I wondered how the message would go down in the islands generally. Afterwards we were all able to shake hands with the Archbishop and his wife Eileen at the door – just like any local parish church service – after which our group of Pilgrims and Philatelists stood with Dr and Mrs Carey for a historic photo-opportunity. We returned to the Upland Goose for lunch to find it awash with foreign correspondents, many of them speaking Spanish.

That afternoon we headed for the Stanley Museum, a fine, spacious wooden edifice whose history was soon explained to us by John Smith, the curator. It had originally been built as the headquarters of the Argentine air link, LADE, with prefabricated sections flown in from Argentina. Then, after the conflict, it was decided by common consent that the building would make an excellent local museum.

Gwerfyl was taken off to inspect early records of past governors, particularly those referring to her ancestor Colonel George D'Arcy. My attention was caught by one surprisingly familiar object: a saddle with distinctive triangular leather stirrups of a type that I had last seen some forty-four years ago across the water in Patagonia. It was one of the indigenous *gaucho* saddles used by shepherds and stockmen all over the Southern Cone of America – and suddenly I felt at home. But what was it doing in Stanley Museum?

I did not dig out the facts until some time later. About sixty *gauchos* arrived in the Falklands in 1844, with a licence to cull the large numbers of wild cattle originating from the animals shipped to the islands by the first French settlers at Port Louis. A number of these men's descendants remained in the islands, working as itinerant cattle-hunters and giving occasional help on the sheep farms as they became established. My grandfather in his younger days would sometimes take a few days out to go hunting with them.

Also on display was a book entitled *74 Days: An Islander's Diary of the Falklands Occupation*. John Smith was the author, so we were able to get our autographed copies on the spot.

The streets were quiet that Sunday evening as I took a stroll round Stanley. Many windows displayed STOP ALL WHALING posters – an ironic post-script to the islands' early history as an important base for the whaling industry. From my vantage-point on Davis Street, I looked down to the harbour. The sun was getting low and there, spanning the water in the quiet of the evening, was the magnificent arch of a double rainbow.

3. WEST FALKLAND

The fine weather still held the next day as we embarked on our next FIGAS flight – this time to West Falkland. We peered out at the contours below, trying to match the jigsaw-like coastline with what we recalled of the map, passing first over Teal Inlet settlement and then San Carlos – unknown to the world at large until the Task Force made its landing there. Next we were crossing Falkland Sound, the stretch of water dividing the two main islands and, almost before we knew it, had touched down on the grassy airstrip at Port Howard. Within five minutes we arrived at the settlement, a group of buildings as large as a small village clustered round a sheltered inlet.

Port Howard, the earliest farm settlement on West Falkland, was established in 1867 by James Lovegrove Waldron, a well-to-do farmer from Peasmore, a village near Newbury in Berkshire. With two other farmers he chartered a ship, the *Diane*, complete with shepherds, servants and 'the necessaries of life for years to come': houses, sheds, implements, horses, cows, thoroughbred rams and ewes and a year's supply of pressed hay. He took up land on the eastern side of the mountains that divide the island.

In the following year two adventurous young men, Wickham Bertrand – Sally Blake's great-grandfather – and Ernest Holmested, arrived and took up land on the western side of the mountains. After a few years Bertrand went off to set up on his own at Roy Cove further west, and Holmested took on a new partner by the name of Robert Blake, my grandfather, who had just arrived in the islands. After years of phenomenally hard work, Ernest Holmested and his family eventually returned to England and Robert Blake became responsible for the running of the farm later known as Hill Cove.

As sheep farming on the islands continued to prosper, Waldron, in common with a number of other farmers, began to look towards the mainland of Argentina where there were opportunities for further development. In 1885 he bought a large tract of land in southern Patagonia bordering on the Magellan Straits and established another farm there. It was called Estancia Condor. Seven years later Blake was arranging to purchase territory further north, inland from the sheltered harbour of San Julián. Initially registered as the San Julián Sheep Farming Company, it later became known as Estancia Coronel. The two families, Blakes and Waldrons, having started off as neighbours and later sharing the problems of settling on the coast of Patagonia, supported one another in many different ways over the years in both personal and business matters.

For this reason I was glad to have the opportunity of visiting Port Howard, a place familiar to me by name from my earliest years. I even possessed a watercolour of a local view, painted by my mother during a visit that she made here with my father during the 1950s. For me, it made a sort of substitute for Hill Cove. We all crowded into the hall of the comfortable house where the manager had once lived and were shown up to our rooms. For all I knew, I might have been in the same one that had been occupied by my parents forty years earlier.

There was no time to speculate on this, however, for we were immediately whisked off by Land-Rover to one of the first events of Sports Week: a barbecue at Harps Farm. By the time we arrived the event was in full swing. People of all ages and sizes were coming and going round the large central barbecue; children were running in and out, a chunk of food in one hand, a plastic cup of drink in the other. There was plenty for everybody, and we, although strangers, were accepted without question. Now that the hard work and tension of shearing time were at an end, there was general contentment and relaxation.

In the afternoon came the sheepdog trials: five sheep to be taken through a gate and herded into a pen. The intelligent dogs ran, crouched, waited, one ear cocked for the whistled signal. The whole business called for a lot of patience. If the dogs did not always do as well as might be expected, it must have been because they were accustomed to moving large numbers of sheep around and not just a paltry five animals. It was all quite time-consuming, and we wandered off to explore some of the rest of the farm.

'Come and have a look at the wool shed,' said Ronnie, our tour leader. 'It's brand-new.' For this was one of the new farms that had been carved out of the former large estate.

'Do you feel at home here, Rosemary?' the others asked me as we went inside.

'Well . . . yes and no,' I said.

The 'yes' was the overwhelming familiarity of the smell of sheep's fleece, which permeates every shearing shed. I had not smelt it for years. The 'no' was to do with the size of the place, so small in comparison with the great long building which my grandfather had helped to build with his own hands far away in Patagonia.

When the time came to return to Port Howard settlement there was a shortage of Land-Rovers, and we managed to make room for two extra passengers. I made a friendly comment to one of the visitors as she squeezed in beside me, but she did not respond because, I realized, she had not understood my words.

'I'm Italian,' she said. I could not quite see how she fitted into this particular picture, but evidently her English was not up to explaining the situation.

'Gwerfyl, look over there!' called Ronnie. 'That's Mount D'Arcy!'

Our passenger seemed nervous – but maybe she was not used to travelling by Land-Rover, whereas we by this time had become quite blasé about it.

'Italian? Nothing of the sort,' said Ronnie when I mentioned it that evening. 'She's Argentine.'

Always one to have his ear to the ground, he told us that she was part of a television crew that had come over from Argentina to film the islanders in their natural habitat so as to present a picture of what they were really like. This was part of an initiative to help Argentines accept the reality of the current situation. It was in effect a clandestine operation, so we all had to keep our mouths shut – but it certainly raised questions as to how the islanders had previously been depicted in the Argentine media. I wondered where the visitors were staying, for since Port Howard was hosting Sports Week this year every house in the rest of the settlement would be full to bursting with people from all the other farms on the island.

That night there was a dance, which a few of us made up our minds to attend. I still retained memories of the dances as my brother described them in the late 1940s and early 1950s, with music provided by an accordion and many of the old traditional dances still vigorously in use. By the time we arrived at the venue it was about 9.30; it would be well under way by now, we thought. But we came into an empty hall to the sound of three amplified guitars just tuning up, and it was clear that nothing was going to be happening for at least another half-hour. We decided in favour of an early night.

Tuesday was a perfect day for the races. We heard the sound of the Islander aircraft coming in to land as we made our way up to the improvised race-course.

'That'll be the Archbishop and his party,' said Ronnie.

We soon met up with Sally and were introduced to Paul, the eldest of the next generation of Falkland Blakes, who would be riding in one of the races. Of Tim, however, there was no sign.

'He's in the tote box,' said Sally. I could then just make out the outline of my cousin inside the small hut, where people were queuing to place their bets for the first race. The names of the horses and their riders were chalked up on a blackboard next to the window. *D. Betts*, read one of the names. He should do well, I thought, for Betts was the name of one of the *gauchos* working on West Falkland in my grandfather's day.

Now the clerical party put in its appearance. The Archbishop, last seen resplendent in cope and mitre at the cathedral door, was dressed for a day at the races with flat cap, storm-proof jacket and purple sweat-shirt with *Falkland Islands Pilgrimage* on it. Cameras came out and were clicking like mad, but Dr Carey had his own camera, too. Suddenly I found myself face to face with the Primate of All England, talking about cameras.

Then there was a shout: the first race had started. Seven horses thundered past and everyone cheered. Over on the other side of the course, meanwhile, were our television friends of yesterday, filming the event for Argentine posterity.

In between races we grouped and regrouped in different combinations, rather like the fragments in a kaleidoscope. The Archbishop sent someone off to place a discreet bet on his behalf, and Mrs Carey won £2. It was a free and easy atmosphere in which you felt you could speak your mind on any topic to anyone you pleased. At one point I found myself in conversation with Colin Bazeley, Bishop in South America, whose episcopal seat was now in Santiago. Our talk turned to the conflict of ten years ago – for Port Howard, unlike Hill Cove on the western side of the mountains, had been one of the farm settlements under Argentine occupation, playing unwilling host to a thousand soldiers and having to slaughter twenty-five sheep a day to feed them.

The Bishop defined the islanders' experience in an unexpected way. 'It was like rape,' he said.

He was right, I thought. John Smith in Stanley had said as much in his diary: 'The town has been raped brutally and without warning, leaving everyone in a deep state of shock.'

How much healing, we as visitors wondered, had taken place over the past ten years?

Another race, however, was now coming up, and this was the big one, the Maiden Plate, with Paul Blake on Victory as one of the contenders. Wearing a red, white and blue football shirt, with the head of red hair he had inherited from his mother, he was not hard to identify. But it was a strong field, with the women competing alongside the men. We all cheered our hardest and in the end Victory, a good-looking chestnut, came second.

Bold Cove is a long inlet running parallel to Port Howard's sheltered harbour, and that afternoon we went to explore it. This was another cross-country run with no track in sight, so that when the Land-Rover got bogged down it was a question of everyone getting out to lighten the load.

'If you do twelve miles an hour by car,' a local once remarked, 'you're doing well.' We could consider ourselves to have been let off easily, in the light of a few of my grandfather's adventures in the early days: 'Coming back from Teal River with some *gauchos*, we tried to find a route over the hills and Holmested missed his way in the fog. All five horses became bogged in the wet camp, and it took us fourteen hours' riding to do the twenty-five miles home.' My grandfather was using the word 'camp' in the Patagonian/Falklands style, meaning 'country' or 'terrain'. It comes directly from the Spanish *campo*.

The plan in any case was for us to walk back to Port Howard, looking at one or two landmarks on the way. It was a welcome chance to stretch our legs and take in the special combination of land and sea so reminiscent of parts of Scotland or Ireland except for the different types of plants and birds. We headed first down to Bold Cove itself, where we could see one of the landmarks standing not far from the shore. It was a plain, waist-high monument of local stone, and we discovered that it commemorated the first documented landing on the islands, by Captain John Strong in 1690.

The shore was a great place for seashells of all kinds, particularly giant mussels and clams. As we left the bay behind, there was a chance to identify some of the plants. In places there were patches of diddle-dee, the ubiquitous low-lying shrub of the islands, whose small red translucent berries – not unlike a redcurrant – were just ripe and ready for picking. Then, to my surprise, we came across green patches of prickly burr such as we used to throw at each other in Patagonia, the trick being to get the burr in the middle of the other person's back just where it could not be reached. It felt a great achievement, too, to be able to identify the distinctive leaves of the spring-flowering Scurvy Grass. Had we been here in the spring we should have seen as well the flowers of the delicate Pale Maiden and the bright yellow Lady's Slipper calceolaria, plants that were familiar to us in Patagonia. Not being a botanist, I was unable to identify any other plants that were common to both sides of the water – but in any case it was impossible to keep walking along nose to the ground, ignoring the wide vistas of rolling country with sea beyond.

We could see our second landmark ahead as we rounded an arm of the bay. It was a small white-painted wooden enclosure, a small graveyard not unlike the local cemetery at Darwin. In addition to the usual selection of headstones, there was a rough wooden cross of very recent date. This was erected in memory of Captain John Hamilton of the Special Air Service, killed in action on 10 June 1982, just three days before the end of the war. He and a signaller were occupying an observation post overlooking Port Howard but were spotted by the occupying Argentine troops and surrounded. Ordering the signaller to escape, Hamilton continued to hold the position until he ran out of ammunition and was killed. The signaller was later captured. This was the only gun battle fought on West Falkland during the entire war, and Hamilton was recommended for a posthumous Victoria Cross. The Argentines were so impressed by his bravery that they asked for – and got – a Union Jack with which to cover his body.

A little further on the buildings of Port Howard came into view, caught in the gleam of the late afternoon sun. We found that we had come full circle and were now back on the racecourse. The final race had been run and the tired horses were being led away. The ecclesiastical visitors had flown back to Stanley, and most people had by now drifted down to the settlement, preparing for another evening's celebration.

Next morning, packed and ready, we sat or lay on the sunny lawn outside the travel lodge, awaiting the arrival of the FIGAS flight that was to take us to Pebble Island. It was not long before we heard the now familiar throb of the approaching aircraft. We knew by this time that our journey round the islands was public knowledge – as indeed were the movements of everyone who travelled by air, for the flights and names of passengers for that day were broadcast every morning on the Falkland Islands Broadcasting Service. It seems that there is still not much you can get up to in the islands without it being known sooner or later by everyone else.

As the Islander headed north, we plunged into a bank of cloud, and for the first time on our stay we were none the wiser as to what was below us on the ground. Pebble Island forms the northern border of West Falkland, and there is no land due north from here until you get to Uruguay and northern Argentina. A brisk wind buffeted us as we climbed out of the plane, and it felt several degrees colder than the sheltered haven of Port Howard. By the time we reached the comfort of the travel lodge, with hot coffee and a welcoming peat fire in the main sitting-room, we realized that we would need another layer of clothing before going out to explore.

A quarter of a mile's walk through a paddock of sturdy Falkland horses brought us to the wide expanse of beach, with the unlimited waters of the South Atlantic rolling up along the shore. Not a creature was in sight except for a single pair of kelp geese on the sea strand, perfectly at home in the middle of all that space. It was enough just to stroll along the beach, collecting shells and responding to the sense of freedom generated by the presence of the open sea.

In the afternoon it was Land-Rover time again and a chance to renew our acquaintance with jackass penguins in their burrows and scores of king cormorants, totally unfazed by our presence, in their cliff-top rookery. As we came down a little closer to the rocky waterline it was a surprise to see people in the water, for nobody does much swimming round the Falklands. Then we realized that these swimmers were non-human and were actually the remainder of a colony of sea lions, many of which had already taken off for deeper waters. After this we moved on to another part of the island, a stretch of wetland that yielded a remarkable variety of birds including the unobtrusive, spindly-legged rufous-chested dotterel and, in the distance, a few of the famous black-necked swans.

It was not, however, a day for hanging about, and the travel lodge seemed particularly welcoming that evening. For the fourteen Pebble Islanders incarcerated here for a month in 1982, it would have been a lot more comfortable than the Goose Green community hall. They were imprisoned after the raid on the night of 14 May when eleven of the Argentine aircraft sitting on the Pebble airstrip were destroyed in a covert Special Air Service operation.

After supper, somebody – I cannot remember who – suggested a game of Monopoly. It turned out to be one of those shared experiences which are quite impossible to describe unless you were actually there. In the words of Deaconess Patti Schmiegelow, who later wrote a report of our trip for the *Falkland Islands Newsletter*: 'Our last two nights out of Stanley were marked by the most vicious and hilarious games of Monopoly I have played in years, both of which ended in sudden and total darkness, as the generators were switched off.' Certainly the game revealed unsuspected talents in members of the party for baseness and skulduggery of all kinds. But, as Patti added on a more serious note, 'I suppose that says a great deal for the friendships that were formed in our brief adventures together.'

Next morning, however, brought a new challenge in the shape of a Force 8 gale. Our first objective was the memorial to HMS *Coventry*, the fourth British ship to be sunk by the Argentine Air Force, as it was patrolling the waters north of the islands. Perched on a rocky knoll overlooking the sea, the memorial was not easy to approach under such conditions. Before we got out, the Land-Rover had to manoeuvre until it was heading straight into the wind. This made the doors harder to open; but had the vehicle been facing the other way an unexpected gust of wind could easily have torn an open door right off its hinges. When it came to taking photographs, it seemed as if you needed an extra hand to anchor yourself firmly in case you were blown off balance. Having survived this challenge, we were just driving away when we heard the sound of a helicopter heading for the airstrip. This, we learnt, was bringing in a military team who had come to inspect the memorial on behalf of the War Graves Commission, in anticipation of the anniversary that would be taking place later in the year.

We then headed for a bare expanse of open cliff-top, advancing cautiously in the teeth of the gale. There ahead of us, huddled close to the ground, their heads tucked into their soft plumage so that they looked like large fluffy whitish eggs, were some twenty birds, each the size of a farmyard fowl. But these were *babies*. They were the chicks of the giant petrel, roosting out in the open in the most uncomfortable conditions it was possible to imagine. It seemed advisable not to go too close, for an encounter with a large and angry parent bird would not have been a good experience.

We turned inland to find a more sheltered spot for lunch.

'This is a great place for wild strawberries,' we were told. Sure enough, careful scanning of the ground revealed the small shiny red berries – actually rather more like a raspberry – which were distinctive and delicious and an unexpected addition to our sandwiches.

After this we drove to Pebble Beach on the southern side of the island. The 'pebbles' after which the island is named are translucent stones that make attractive jewellery, as I knew from a pair of earrings once given to me by my father. With the waves pounding the shore behind us, we spent about twenty minutes bent double, searching among the shingle for the tell-tale gleam of the elusive stones, finding enough between us to prove that they really did exist.

'That's Keppel Island over there, by the way,' said Ronnie. 'I was hoping we might get a boat across to it, but it's too windy.' I stared across the water at the island that had such a remarkable history as the launching pad for the evangelization of the Indians of Tierra del Fuego.

It was in 1853 that representatives of the Patagonian Missionary Society arrived on Keppel Island to establish a base from which to mount expeditions to the remote lands south of the Magellan Straits. During the following years, small groups of Yahgan Indians were brought to the mission centre to accustom them to a simple European farming lifestyle. Governor D'Arcy, who visited the island in 1871, described Keppel as 'a little Arcadian settlement' and the Indians as 'a quiet, intelligent race, much attached to their English catechists'. The Indians were then taken back to Tierra del Fuego to form the nucleus of mission settlements there.

None of this would have been possible had someone not taken the trouble to learn the Indians' own language: a young man by the name of Thomas Bridges, who arrived in 1856 at the age of thirteen with the family of the Reverend George Despard. Five years later, when Despard returned to England, Bridges remained at the mission station.

'Among the few Yahgans who were left behind,' wrote his son Lucas, 'were a married couple, Okoko, who had been baptized by the name of George, and his wife, Gamela . . . My father worked, and practically lived, with them, listening to their continuous chatter, for they were a talkative and laughter-loving pair. In this way he was able to unravel the mysteries of their intricate yet beautiful grammar.'

By the time Despard's successor, the Reverend Whait Stirling, arrived a year later, Thomas Bridges was fluent in the Yahgan language and had begun to compile a dictionary. In September 1871, after ordination in England, he arrived in Ushuaia, Tierra del Fuego, with his wife and baby daughter, to begin his life's work in the uttermost part of the earth.

The Keppel mission centre, together with its ship, the *Allen Gardiner* – named after the Society's first missionary, who had died in Tierra del Fuego – also provided inestimable support for the new farmers just getting established on West Falkland. The 88-ton schooner plied regularly between Stanley and West Falkland, carrying passengers, stores, building materials, wool and anything else that needed transporting. Ernest Holmested in particular valued the welcome he always received from the Bartlett family who looked after the mission station. He felt at home there from his first visit in July 1868, when he enjoyed a snowball fight with the ten resident Indians and went rabbiting with young Thomas Bridges.

Keppel Island continued as a training centre and base of missionary operations until 1898, when the last Indians were taken back to Tierra del Fuego. After this the settlement was run as a farm on behalf of the South American Missionary Society, as it was now called, until the island was sold to Dean Brothers of Pebble Island in 1911.

The weather next morning took a turn for the better, but now we were bound back for Stanley. It was our last day in the Islands: a time of final purchases and last-minute photography. I had a special date with a Stanley resident, Madge McPhee, whom I had met at the cathedral the previous Sunday. She hoped I would have time to drop in for a cup of tea before I left, and I was able to find her house in John Street without difficulty. No one stands on ceremony in the Falklands, and soon we were talking away as if I had been visiting since the year dot. After all the sightseeing and special events, I really valued this opportunity to meet and chat with a local person in her own home.

In the evening there was a farewell party at Malvina House, the hotel where the other half of the group had been staying. A number of prominent citizens were present – we did not know who they all were – and I, meanwhile, found myself having a quiet conversation in Spanish with a young woman who turned out to be from Chile. She deplored the fact, on a purely personal level, that there was so little communication between the Falklands and their continental neighbours, and we found ourselves in agreement on a number of issues. If only the politics could be removed from the situation, increased communication at a grassroots level could only be beneficial for all concerned. At the same time, it was important to appreciate what the islanders had been through, and their wishes had to be respected. Maybe, as time went on, more positive links might develop between the Islands and the mainland – as, indeed, had existed during the early pioneering years . . . I was relieved to find that my Spanish was not as rusty as I had thought.

At mid-morning the following day – 29th February – our TriStar took off from Mount Pleasant. I found myself sitting next to an agreeable young man just returning from his tour of duty in the islands, his assignment being surveillance and communication. I got the impression that the job involved a fair amount of boredom – but this, after all, had to be one of the two extremes of any military career. As with all return journeys the eighteen hours seemed to pass much more quickly than the outward trip. Early next morning we were touching down at Brize Norton and there was Rick, who had had to get up at a most unreasonable hour, waiting to drive us home.

The following week I rang Gwerfyl to find out how she was re-acclimatizing to the northern hemisphere.

'Oh, not too bad,' she said. 'But now I know why it was that the children were so keen to get me out of the way.'

During the two weeks of her absence, they had completely redecorated her kitchen.

4. BUENOS AIRES

'Wouldn't you like to go back to Patagonia?'

I had been asked that question more than once over the years and never quite knew how to reply. My visit to the Falklands, it was true, had taken me back into the southern hemisphere – but geographical proximity counted for nothing in the current political climate. Meanwhile, both Eleanor and Hugh had made the trip back to Patagonia. But maybe I did not need to go; maybe George, in 1982, had done the journey on my behalf. I was well aware, through my brother and sister-in-law, as well as my nieces and nephews, how much Argentina had changed since I had said goodbye to our farm at the age of eleven. It went without saying that I had changed, too. My experience of the country was based on the limited, intensely personal perspective of childhood; I had reached adulthood in Britain and had become reintegrated into the British way of life. After so many years would I and the country where I was born still have anything to say to each other?

Hispanic influences, however, were filtering into our life from another quarter. Our daughter Maggie, who had gone to teach English in Madrid, ended up with a Spanish husband, none of whose family spoke a word of English. I found myself once again getting immersed in the Spanish language so as to be able to hold my own at González family gatherings.

'What language,' enquired José's mother, 'do they speak in the Malvinas?'

'English,' I said firmly. She seemed surprised.

Then, in 1998, around the time of our fortieth wedding anniversary, I received a telephone call from my nephew Stuart, now living in London.

'I'm embarrassed,' he said. 'It's happened again!'

'What has?'

'The Anglo-Argentine Society's annual raffle. This is the second time I've won first prize. Two return flights to Argentina!'

'What a bit of luck!'

'Yes, but we can't use them: it's the wrong time of year for us. Would you like them?'

How could we refuse?

There was a lot of groundwork to be done first. This was not just a trip round the tourist sites; it was a journey back into my own past and had to be carefully thought through. I decided that I would be travelling, as it were, on my mother's passport, for these were the connections with which I was most familiar.

John, of course, was delighted by the news and offered the use of the family flat in Buenos Aires. He was not, however, optimistic about our chances of being able to revisit the farm, even if we did get to San Julián. On the other hand, I reflected, on-the-spot information might give a different picture. I wrote another letter, this time to an address in Shropshire. The response was warm and immediate.

'How nice to hear from you; and lovely to hear that you have the chance to go back to the Argentine,' wrote Bessie Pearce, who had helped to look after me when I was a little girl. She gave me the addresses of three of her sisters, Cath Mann and Mary and Lidia Pickering, who were brought up at Coronel and still lived in San Julián. But before I even had time to write, two letters arrived, one from Cath and one from Mary, welcoming us and inviting us to stay.

Mary's letter contained a series of snapshots that were over fifty years old: farewell photos taken on 12 March 1947 of my father and mother, Hugh, Eleanor and myself, standing on the beach, with the coastal steamer *Asturiano* waiting behind us in the bay. Those tiny pictures, from so far away and long ago, made an instant connection. There was my eleven-year-old self, my teenage brother and sister, my mother with her 1940s' pompadour hairstyle, my father shaking hands in his characteristically energetic way. And there were all the friends and neighbours with whom we shared our lives, who had come to bid us farewell. I had the photos enlarged and sent copies to Hugh and Eleanor so that they might feel connected, too.

I wrote to my old friend Agnes Mann, who also showed up in one of the snapshots and was now living in Montevideo; I hoped that there might be a chance to meet up with her during our stay in Buenos Aires. A long catching-up letter came back – but clearly there would not be time to allow for a dash across the River Plate into Uruguay. Never mind; at least we were in touch.

There was another link with the past to be followed up. This was Raquel, an old friend of my mother's, who had re-established contact with John and his family some years previously. When John had provided me with the address, I wrote to her.

'Was I surprised!' came her reply – 'but how glad to hear from you. The years have flown – but friendship does not depend on time or distance . . . Everything is changed – nevertheless some of us old people are still the same . . . *Hasta pronto!*' So now, it was clear, a visit to Raquel would be included in our journey.

A fourth letter was faxed to a complete stranger in Tierra del Fuego. We had decided that, since we were travelling so far, it would be a pity not to go the full distance to the southernmost tip of the continent. As luck would have it, the previous year my sister had attended a conference where she was delighted to meet someone from Argentina. Eleanor had the visitor to stay, and they became good friends. Since Lilián was living in Tierra del Fuego, we hoped to reinforce this long-distance connection.

We spent a day with Stuart and his young family for a full-scale briefing on all the practical details: addresses, telephone numbers, the location of the flat in Buenos Aires, even the names of friendly restaurants. We acquired a detailed up-to-date handbook of the country, as well as masses of brochures from Aerolíneas Argentinas. Letters and faxes shuttled backwards and forwards between Britain and Argentina as the itinerary gradually took shape.

Then, two weeks before our departure, a fax arrived from John. He had received disturbing news: Mary had been admitted to hospital in Gallegos for an emergency operation for cancer.

I rang Bessie in Shropshire, guessing that she would have the latest information.

'Yes, she's had the operation; it looks as if they caught it in time. Cath and Lidia are both in Gallegos at the moment. We're all in touch; we've always been a very close family.'

We decided that this setback was not going to stop us travelling to San Julián, even though we did not know what we should find when we got there.

And so, six months after Stuart's surprise telephone call, there we were on a jumbo jet bound for Buenos Aires. It was 28 February 1999 – seven years, almost to the day, since I had returned from the Falklands.

The flight from Heathrow to Madrid was conducted in impeccable European style. When, however, my husband Jeremy and I boarded the plane for Buenos Aires, taking off just before midnight, it felt as if we had walked straight into South America. People were relaxed and cheerful, sitting where they liked, smoking wherever they wanted – and, of course, everyone conversed with each other. We saw the dawn break as we were coming over Brazil, south of Rio, and I reminded Jeremy to look north for the sun. A round of applause broke out when we touched down at Buenos Aires.

Everything looked so much greener than the austere mountains round Madrid, with tall plumes of pampas grass growing freely – this being, after all, their natural habitat.

I held my breath as we reached passport control. Would they notice the Falkland Islands visa stamped in my passport, and, if so, would anything happen? I recalled my landing at Mount Pleasant airport in 1992; the authorities had been very polite as they searched my suitcase thoroughly. But here in Buenos Aires no one batted an eyelid, and I passed straight through.

On our way to John's and Monica's flat I was on the look-out for familiar features. Some of the street names I still remembered – but the first recognition came with the sight of the cobbled streets and the patterned paving stones over which I used to drag my heels to make a nice noise and get told off for it. As the taxi drew up at the apartment block I prepared my best Spanish: 'Good morning, I'm John Blake's sister; could I please have the key to the flat?' None of this was necessary. The porter merely said, 'The key's just coming': we had been recognized immediately. We were shown to the lift for the nineteenth floor and hauled our luggage through the door of the pleasant, spacious apartment that was to be our home for the next few days. From the balcony one could see all over high-rise Buenos Aires and as far as the mud-coloured River Plate in the north.

Our first need was to get cool and change into the lightweight summer gear appropriate to this sub-tropical climate. After that we had to sort out our financial situation, which involved taking a taxi to Calle Tucumán to change dollars. Our first impressions of Buenos Aires recalled both Madrid and Paris, but some of the older areas were quite shabby now, although softened by the wonderful greenery of the mature trees. Here, it seemed, was a city relaxed and at ease with itself. There were the old familiar streets – Maipú, so narrow, hopelessly congested with traffic – but Lavalle, where all the cinemas used to be, had been pedestrianized. We took the Subterráneo back. It was good to get reacquainted with the underground railway system, which was spacious and well organized, even if the routes were limited. We had just enough energy to prepare a meal and fall into bed. In the night there was a typical tropical thunderstorm and downpour.

(Animal note: large pampered dogs being taken for walks by paid helpers; thin feral felines in the Botanical Gardens; and two young pigeons being fed by their mother on the balcony of the flat.)

Next day – fresher after the rain – we continued to unravel the mysteries of the Subterráneo, eventually getting as far as Plaza San Martín. I had an early memory of the Plaza, with its vendors of children's toys: birds on a string that whistled as you swung them round. Now the Plaza had grown up but was remarkably beautiful, with exotic trees in flower and a terrace where you could lean on the balustrade and look down towards the river. There, just in front of us, was the British Clock Tower, dominating what until the Falklands War was called the Plaza Británica but which was renamed Plaza de la Fuerza Aérea (Air Force Square).

Then we went on down to Retiro, the once great long-distance railway terminus where, in the winter holidays, we used to catch the overnight sleeper west to Córdoba and the foothills of the Andes. The building now was just a vast echoing space. Next door the suburban network that used to be so familiar was reduced to two or three truncated lines. The railway network, originally set up by the British, had been taken over by the state in Perón's time. Increased road and air traffic had played their part in what was no doubt an inevitable decline.

Near by a grassy green space with a miniature railway seemed to be all that was left of the great Parque Retiro funfair. Where, I wondered, was the amphitheatre – somewhere near there, I thought – where the British community gathered together and sang 'O God Our Help in Ages Past' to celebrate the end of the Second World War in 1945? A heartfelt occasion: I could still remember it after all these years. Amphitheatre? I recalled an enclosure surrounded by a yellowish wall. Would it have been part of the amusement park?

I was glad to discover that my Spanish was proving equal to the occasion. I found it easier to tune in to the language as it was spoken here than the Spanish of the Iberian peninsula and had no difficulty, either, in making myself understood. I got into the habit of passing the time of day with the people with whom we shared the lift; you can hold quite a conversation when you are going up or down nineteen floors.

'Your Spanish is very good,' they would say, charmingly. This, I realized, was code for: 'You don't speak like a native. Where are you from?'

'I was born in Buenos Aires, and I've come back after over fifty years. It's great to be here.'

'Isn't that nice!' they said. 'Have a good stay.'

In the evening came three phone calls: John from Gallegos, Raquel's daughter in Buenos Aires and Lilián from Tierra del Fuego, all making contact and linking us in to this part of the world.

The 3rd of March brought a fresh, clear, breezy morning. Jeremy said he had now accepted that the sun was in the north: an important experience for Europeans. It takes time to adapt to another continent, let alone another hemisphere.

Our first objective was the Plaza de Mayo, full of wind and pigeons and children playing. The headscarves of the Madres – the Mothers of the Disappeared – were painted on the ground, in a circle round the obelisk in front of the presidential palace, together with the outlines of some bodies, representing the 30,000 who had disappeared between 1976 and 1981 during the 'dirty war'. There were also circles enclosing a military cap, with the words: JUICIO – CASTIGO (Judgement – Punishment). Unofficial graffiti included a huge eye with two tears: Rachel weeping for her children . . . It was strange to think that what had begun as a desperate and indeed dangerous quest for the truth, against overwhelming odds, seemed now to have been reduced to a series of pavement graffiti, merely an attraction for inquisitive tourists. But at least the images were there for all to see – and even if justice had only partly been done there had been some acknowledgement of responsibility.

During the World Cup, held in Argentina in 1978, an estimated 367 people disappeared in the run-up to the event and about forty-six during the competition itself. But while the football fans were cheering on the home team – most of them, like the rest of the country, blissfully ignorant of what was happening in their own backyard – the outside world was just beginning to wake up to what was going on in the prisons and interrogation centres. The Dutch team, instead of attending the opening ceremony, elected to come and spend time with the Mothers, and pictures of the women appeared on Dutch television.

'We discovered,' said one of the Mothers, 'that outside Argentina there were people prepared to listen to us. That was the year the support groups began.'

Why the Dutch? I asked myself. History provided the answer. Holland had been an occupied country during the Second World War – and someone next day was to describe Argentina's military regime as *hitleriano*. So it was not difficult for the Dutch to empathize with the Mothers' experiences and to realize the importance of bringing their plight to the attention of the world.

After that the extremely opulent cathedral was something of an anticlimax spiritually, but we gave to two beggars, a man and a woman, outside. We learnt later that it had closed its doors to the Mothers fleeing the tear gas attacks of the police during the first demonstrations in the Plaza in 1977.

Next we walked down Calle San Martín, which gave us an opportunity to look for the old Phoenix Hotel. A few blocks down I thought I had located the site: long closed, derelict, to let. However, as we reached the Avenida de Córdoba, there it was: three-star and very much a going concern. I tried to peer in through the door, and a porter came forward to open it, but I turned away, with an odd feeling as if I had been just about to walk into my past. I then recalled that 'Avenida de Córdoba' had sounded familiar, as if something good was located there. Parents giving directions to taxi-drivers as we got off the boat . . .

The Phoenix Hotel was always, as long as I could remember, our base when we stayed in Buenos Aires. It used to be known as the British Museum on account of the number of elderly British residents holed up there, and in later years our parents, when they returned without us to Argentina, chose a different hotel. But for us children the faded grandeur of the place was all part of the wonder of the Great Metropolis. I never failed to be impressed by the enormous chandeliers in the dining-room, reflected into infinity by the mirrors all round the walls. At night the trams – long since gone – went rattling down Calle San Martín, their lights flickering through the slats of the window-shutters, and in the morning there was the sing-song call of the newspaper vendors: '*La Razón, Crítica, Prensa, Diario-o-o!*' . . . *La Prensa* was the first of the newspapers to be banned, in Perón's day; others, later, came and went.

And across the Avenida on the other side was Harrods – or rather what had once been Harrods: vast and empty like Retiro station . . . *Sic transit*! So we went on down San Martín and eventually got to Florida, now fully pedestrianized. We celebrated our arrival with a drink in a classic pavement café. There at last, too, we located a post office and a place selling postcards – and a vegetarian restaurant.

I was awakened from my siesta by the phone and a deep voice speaking excellent English. It was some time before I realized it was not a man but Raquel herself. 'My voice went years ago, with all the teaching!' she said. She had fixed everything up connected with our visit to her in Comodoro, and she also gave us the phone number of her younger brother Julito, now living in Buenos Aires. While we were debating when to suggest seeing him he rang up, full of affection, and arranged to call in next day. I recalled the attractive little boy, just a few years younger than myself, whom we always considered spoilt because he was allowed, Hispanic style, to stay up until all hours and we were not.

Julito arrived next morning at eleven: tall, now balding, but with the unmistakable dark, rather mournful eyes of his mother. We shared photographs, checked out on memories; there was a great flow of warmth and kindness.

One historic photo showed his father – Don Julio, as we always knew him – with Saint-Exupéry at San Julián.

Antoine de Saint-Exupéry, writer and poet, was one of the team of pilots who in the 1920s established the first airline down the eastern coast of

Patagonia; his classic, *Vol de Nuit*, is a fictionalized account of that remarkable enterprise. Raquel's and Julito's grandmother, a spirited Frenchwoman, gave a warm welcome to the pilots whenever they touched down at San Julián.

'They would arrive in their leather flying-suits and goggles,' she once told Raquel, 'exhausted and chilled to the bone. They called me "Grandmère" and I would give them mulled wine. Later your father and I would help them to wrap their arms and legs in layers of paper, for the leather was no protection against the intense cold. The cockpits were open and the airplanes had no heating except for oval-shaped copper containers filled with blocks of solid alcohol. These were the great men who opened up the air routes, with great risk and sacrifice.'

Julito took us out to lunch. As we talked, the names began to filter back into my mind: the people who had been living in San Julián those fifty-odd years ago, to whom in the intervening years I had scarcely given a thought. Memory by memory, the small seaport town was starting to come to life.

Julio Aloyz, Julito's father, had started work as a *peón* on our family farm in the early days when my Uncle Robert was the manager, but he was soon promoted to the more responsible job of storekeeper. After some years he left to run his own accountancy business in San Julián and was always a familiar figure in the little town. More than once, in the troubled 1920s, he provided crucial assistance in times of crisis on the farm. The two families always remained friends, and when my mother arrived on the scene she took a particular interest in Julio's intelligent young daughter Raquel, which grew into a lasting friendship.

As we trawled through the memories of those earlier days I was able to clarify one or two misconceptions.

'Was it true,' Julito asked, 'that at the Company's [as the farm was known] food rationing was practised, in order to be in sympathy with wartime rationing in Britain?'

'Not at all,' I replied, rather puzzled. Thinking about it later, I realized that he was probably tapping into his father's memories of life on the farm during the First World War, when he was the storekeeper and my uncle had felt it necessary to run a tight ship and not indulge in undue extravagance. Family food during the Second World War, as I recalled it, might have been of a simple English style, but there was always plenty of it.

'Your family and mine', said Julito as we parted, 'were the founders of San Julián.'

In the afternoon we took a walk through Palermo Park. I remembered it as a vast place, the venue for the great national agricultural shows where, in

1936, 1939 and 1940, our own sheep from Coronel carried off prizes. But I was looking for the part I remembered best: the ornamental pond with the pedal-boats and the bicycles for hire where, aged seven, I struggled to keep those two wheels balanced, under the shade of the eucalyptus trees – but it was not to be found. In the evening we returned to Calle Florida and then on down to Retiro in an attempt to locate the old Balneario, the waterfront which I recalled as being near the docks. It must have disappeared years ago: huge roads and buildings blocked our way.

We visited the Malvinas memorial at the bottom end of Plaza San Martín. The eternal flame was burning at one end of a long panel containing lists and lists of names. The fact that they were not in alphabetical order scandalized my orderly British soul. I thought of that other much smaller memorial with British names on it standing on the waterfront at Port Stanley and the neat, white-painted enclosure on the windswept hillside near Goose Green. Officially 746 Argentine troops died in the war, including the 368 who went down in the *General Belgrano*. Britain lost 255 men. To this number, however, had to be added the tally of those whose names were not recorded on any war memorial: the ones who committed suicide during the years after the conflict. By the year 2002, according to the South Atlantic Medal Association support group, more British war veterans had died in this way than had been killed in action.

On our return, there was another telephone call from John to say that he had been invited to the reception for the Prince of Wales in Buenos Aires the following Thursday.

The next day, 5 March, we left the comfort of the flat and set out on the first leg of our journey south. Our first stop was the Welsh colony of Trelew.

5. TRELEW

Trelew means 'Lew's town' and is called after the energetic Lewis Jones who, besides being one of the founding fathers of the Welsh colony, was responsible for bringing railway transport to this part of northern Patagonia. The line was laid in 1886 and led to the development of both Trelew and Madryn, those names that were so familiar to all of us who travelled back and forth along the eastern seaboard. For the rest of the British settlers in Argentina – mostly English and Scots but English-speakers all – this self-contained Welsh enclave always had a certain mystery. Nobody knew very much about it, mainly because of the perplexing language barrier. For it is disconcerting, if you are an Anglo-Argentine, to come across someone whose ruddy complexion and style of clothing mean that he is obviously British – and then discover that you can only communicate with him in Spanish.

It is a fact, however, that as far as many people in Britain are concerned the word Patagonia has only one association: the Welsh colony. And so, since we had come so far already, it seemed a good idea to have a look at the area for ourselves and learn something about it. The history, we soon discovered, is impressive.

Europeans tend to forget that 28 July in the Antipodes is the middle of winter. On this day, in every Welsh chapel along the valley of the Chubut River, there is a tea-party to celebrate 'Gwyl y Glaniad', the day in 1865 that the first colonists landed on the coast, all in their Sunday best. The ship that brought them, charmingly named *Mimosa*, deposited these 152 souls – forty-three men, thirty-two women and seventy-three children – in midwinter on this barren, treeless shore and sailed away.

'The visionary scheme of a Welsh Utopia, in pursuit of which these unfortunate emigrants settled themselves, ought not to be encouraged, likely as it is to end in the starvation of the victims to it. Had it not been for the charity of the Argentine government, this must have been their fate ere now,' remarked the adventurous George Musters, as he travelled through the region with a group of Indians four years later. But there were two or perhaps three reasons why these people, unlike so many other ill-fated expeditions in this part of the world, were able to survive in such an inhospitable land. The first was that there were a number of caves along the coast in which they sheltered during the worst of the winter. The second was that the local Indians took pity on them, providing them with food and essential survival skills, as Musters was able to testify. 'Jackechan (the local chief) described to me that he had seen the settlers "eating grass" and had taught some of them how to hunt and furnished them with *bolas*.'

The *bolas*, the traditional hunting weapon, consisted of a strip of rawhide, at each end of which was fastened a stone. Holding one end in his hand, the hunter – often but not always on horseback – whirled the weapon round his head and let fly. If properly aimed, the *bolas* entangled themselves round the quarry's legs and brought it to the ground.

The third reason for the settlers' survival was that, like the Pilgrim Fathers of North America almost 250 years before them, they were a deeply religious group, and one should never underestimate the power of prayer. The comparison is not a superficial one. The Pilgrim Fathers set sail for New England in 1621 in search of freedom: the freedom to practise their religious beliefs without interference from established church or state. The Welsh came to Patagonia for exactly the same reason, except that what was at stake in their case was their culture and their language. The British government of the day was busy setting up a national education system that actively discouraged minority cultures. How could the Welsh language and tradition survive under such circumstances? To this determined group of people emigration seemed the only solution. But where were they to go? So many of the new territories then opening up to Europeans seeking their fortunes, such as the United States, Canada or Australia, were dominated by the English language. They needed to find a country that was sympathetic to their problem.

There was, as it happened, one country that had once almost become a part of the burgeoning British Empire but which had succeeded in fighting off the challenge to its independence: Argentina. Its government at that time was anxious to encourage new European immigrants to settle the vast tracts of Patagonia and was therefore more than happy to give this group permission to settle in an area that no one in their right mind would ever wish to inhabit.

Caves, friendly Indians and prayers notwithstanding, the colonists had a tough time. The valley of the Chubut River, the area that had been allocated to them, was far from being the green and fertile place it is today. They did find the river after a forty-mile trek, but the landscape through which it flowed was no different from the rest of the treeless semi-desert through which they had been trudging. However, they turned to and established the first settlement of the colony, calling it Rawson, after the government minister with whom the agreement to settle had first been made.

The first two years tested their resources to the utmost, for there was no mistaking the hostility of the environment. Even the river, so essential to survival in that thirsty land, could turn at a moment's notice into a raging torrent, sweeping away the hard-won harvest. Some settlers, indeed, did give up and go home. But at this point somebody had a bright idea: Rachel Jones, the wife of Aaron Jenkins, suggested irrigation as a means of controlling the erratic water-flow.

Irrigation being the key to the whole enterprise, a network of channels began to spring up along the lower part of the Chubut valley. There is no record of Indians being conscripted to do the heavy labour: the work was shared out among the settlers themselves on a cooperative basis. The local Indians were predominantly Tehuelches, who roamed the southern part of Patagonia as far as the Magellan Straits, and not the warlike Araucanos from further north. For many years they coexisted peacefully with the settlers, hunting as they had always done and exchanging their surplus game – guanaco (the Patagonian llama) or ostrich (the small, dun-coloured *Rhea darwinii*) – for farm-made butter and bread. George Musters, who spent the year 1869 travelling northwards with a group of Tehuelches from Punta Arenas to Patagones, describes an encounter with the Indians from the Chubut area:

> Two days after the arrival of the Northern party the Indians from the Chupat came in ... They habitually seemed to have kept more to the sea-coast, where many of them had been accustomed to visit the Welsh colony at the Chupat for trade, and in their opinion, as afterwards expressed to me, the honest Welsh colonists were much pleasanter and safer to deal with than 'the Christians' of the Río Negro. They seemed to have been especially impressed with the size and excellence of the home-made loaves, one of which would be given in return for half a guanaco, and Jackechan often expatiated on the liberality of the colonists and the goodness of their bread. These men also felt strongly the kindness with which an Indian, if overtaken with rum, would be covered up or carried into an outhouse by the Chupat people; whereas at the Río Negro the only attention paid to him would be to strip and plunder him completely.

Idyllic though this scenario might seem, it was not enough by itself to ensure the continuance of the isolated colony. In less than ten years numbers had dwindled to about a hundred. So Abraham Matthews, one of the leaders of the community, went on a mission, travelling both to Wales and the United States in search of reinforcements. In 1874 the second wave of eighty-four settlers arrived, just as the first shipload of the colony's home-grown wheat, the guarantee of economic survival, was being dispatched to Buenos Aires. There were now enough people to build another village a few miles further up the Chubut River. They called it Gaimán, and, now that the enterprise was viable, more groups arrived in successive years.

Later on, a few of the more adventurous trekked three hundred miles across the waterless land to the fertile foothills of the Andes where, in 1888, they were given a further grant of the valley they called Cwm Hyfryd. Here they established the towns of Trevelín (Place by the Mill) and Esquel.

John Pilkington, the 'Englishman in Patagonia', defines the situation in which these new settlers now found themselves.

Although well east of the main *cordillera*, Cwm Hyfryd's waters flow to the Pacific. With the Chilean frontier still, in 1888, very much undecided, the arrival of the Welsh didn't go unnoticed in Santiago. Had the Argentines the power to grant land rights in disputed territory? The matter cast a shadow over the growing community until 1902, when Sir Thomas Holdich's boundary commission turned up and invited the settlers to decide for themselves. The Chileans tried to lure them with land, but the prudent Welsh threw in their lot with their compatriots in the Chubut Valley. They would be Argentine.

Once the essentials for living had been secured, it became possible to attend to the community's cultural life and the maintenance of the Welsh language. The first newspaper, *Ein Breiniad* (*Our Heritage*), made its appearance in 1878, along with the first school textbooks, following the setting up of a printing press. By this time, too, the annual *eisteddfod*, the traditional festival of poetry and song, had become a regular event in the life of the community; it continues to this day. And one by one, strung out along the Chubut valley, sprang up the chapels: Bethel, Ebenezer, Carmel, Glan Alaw, Bethesda, Bryn Crwn, Salem, Seion, Bethlehem, Nazareth, Tabernacl and Moriah.

Aeroparque Jorge Newbery, Buenos Aires's internal airport, is in a pleasant area alongside the River Plate, further upstream. We could see what looked like a riverside walk – a replacement, perhaps, for the old Balneario we had been trying to find the night before.

We took off from here at midday. The last time my sister and I had flown from Buenos Aires, in December 1946, going home for the summer holidays, was before sunrise, the lights still twinkling from the little farms.

From the 1930s onwards Aeroposta Argentina, the airline established by Saint-Exupéry and his team, became the regular way to travel up and down the eastern coast of Patagonia and the way we always went to and from boarding-school. The planes were sixteen-seater Junkers, with a speed of 150 miles an hour. They hopped from port to port, calling at Bahía Blanca, Trelew, Comodoro, Deseado, San Julián, Santa Cruz and Río Gallegos. At every stop you got out and walked across to the airport building where, if it was time for a meal, a cold buffet was set out on a long table. Whether you felt like eating or not depended on the smoothness of the flight. The worst part was always over Comodoro, where the updraughts from the oil wells caused the plane to buck like a frisky horse; if you kept a level stomach there, you could keep it anywhere. These stops, which must have lasted anything up to an hour, added considerably to the journey time: from Buenos Aires to San Julián, for example, took twelve hours. But since the only alternative was the ten-day boat journey, the coast road not having been built yet, we did not think of it as a hardship.

The flight this time was only a hop of one hour forty minutes. At last, there was the coastline of Patagonia stretching down to the south: blue sea, vast tracts of empty land, familiar dun-coloured terrain. Suddenly we were out at sea, crossing the great Golfo San Matías: what a feeling, looking south towards the Pole, all that expanse of water, the old explorers' excitement . . . At this point Jeremy, biting on a crusty sandwich, lost a front tooth.

Now we were coming down to land at Trelew – the unmistakable mottled surface of the land rising up to meet us – and at last setting foot on the ground of Patagonia, after all these years.

It was only a short walk to the cosy little airport, plonked down in the middle of the wilderness, where we found a friendly taxi-driver who told us all about Trelew, which had now mushroomed to 90,000 inhabitants. At the Residencia Rivadavia the *señora*, just as the handbook had said, proved very helpful, providing us with a map of the town. We had no problem in finding the bus station and booking the tickets to our next stop at Comodoro. Then, feeling peckish, we located the Touring Club Hotel: spacious, old-fashioned, comfortable, where we were able to obtain large cups of tea and toasted cheese sandwiches. The place had evidently changed very little since John Pilkington's visit ten years previously, travelling northwards on the last leg of his journey through Patagonia:

On shelves behind the bar were ranged a hundred spirit bottles. Some clearly hadn't been opened in years. Their murky contents lurked poisonously behind mould-covered glass, waiting for the day when an innocent traveller might point across the bar and order a shot. Above this collection a clock counted the seconds with loud, measured ticks which echoed from wall to wall. Otherwise the tearoom was silent.

Trelew's very wide streets made it feel, as Jeremy said, like a Wild West frontier town – although this was slightly belied by the presence of several high-rise buildings. We noticed also – something we did not see in any other town we visited – the numbers of indigenous Indians going about their ordinary business just like everyone else. It appeared to be a measure of the way the Welsh related to them: mutual respect. As we explored the town we saw notices in some of the shop windows – in Spanish – inviting people to join the local choral society.

Then we went in search of St David's, the English-based school of which my father had once been a governor. We located the St David's Association social centre and had a long chat in Spanish with the man at the information office, who told us what he knew, which was not much, since the school had disappeared years ago. He himself was Welsh on both sides – Roberts and Jones – and had been on a Welsh study course at Lampeter. He directed us to where the school had been: a surprisingly small private house.

The last good experience of the day was our evening meal at Casa Juan, in what must have been an early Welsh house, where there was a warm and welcoming atmosphere.

A photographic session the following morning led us back to the site of St David's school, where we discovered what had evidently been the back entrance. We realized that it must once have occupied a much bigger area that had later been built over.

Then we took the bus to Gaimán. As we trundled out of Trelew we were able to see where many of the 90,000 inhabitants were housed. The suburban streets soon gave way to shanty dwellings, growing more and more makeshift the further out of town we got, and we could see that the population in this part was predominantly Indian. At last, however, Trelew was behind us and we were travelling through the real dry, dusty Patagonian landscape, although off to the left we could see the poplars and greenery which marked the valley of the Chubut River. We assumed that the bus was going only to Gaimán, but the next thing we knew it had gone through it and was coming into Dolavon, so we got off there, which was just as well, because this was the westernmost of the coastal Welsh settlements. Between Dolavon and the two towns of Esquel and Trevelín in the foothills of the Andes lay three hundred miles of sparsely populated terrain, the vast

Patagonian hinterland. Many mysteries were still concealed here: one just coming to light, we learnt later, was an extraordinary prehistoric phenomenon, a vast dinosaur graveyard. So little of significance had taken place between those times and our own that the site had for aeons lain undisturbed and was only now yielding archaeological information of unprecedented importance.

We were quite relieved, however, not to have ended up in the middle of nowhere. After a stroll round the neat suburban streets of Dolavon and discovering what later turned out to be a chapel built over the irrigation canal, we were directed by the kind lady at the garage where to catch the bus, and so returned to Gaimán.

There were enough of the old brick-built houses here to ensure that some of the charm of the place still remained. Additional attractions for tourists were the *casas de té*, offering tea and home-made cakes in a traditional British setting – something of a novelty for people of Spanish or Italian origin. We crossed the Chubut River by the old footbridge, which still remained alongside the existing one, and found a peaceful path along the riverbank.

Eventually it was time to visit Plas y Coed, the oldest of the several Welsh teahouses. As it was near the end of the season we were the only ones there and were served by the niece of Marta Rees, the doyenne of the place. Eventually we got to talk in English with Marta herself, and she had many reminiscences of the early days, being descended from one of the original colonists. After the death of her mother, however, she had been brought up in the Boer community near Comodoro.

To begin with I rather confusedly thought this meant that she had been to South Africa, for this was the first I had heard of the Dutch colonists who had emigrated to Patagonia in the aftermath of the Boer War. As practised settlers, they knew how to establish themselves in an undeveloped country, and they had certain things in common with the Welsh: a desire to retain their own language, a sturdy, Bible-based type of Protestantism and a marked dislike of the English. This mutual sympathy evidently extended to helping one another out in times of family crisis.

When I said that Comodoro was our next port of call and mentioned Raquel's name – oh yes, she knew her! We enjoyed talking with Marta, who came across as a strong, humorous personality.

Then Billie, Marta's niece, drove us on a tour of the town, starting with the two chapels, the old original and the larger one built in 1913. We learnt that, as in most of Europe, it was now usually only the older people who attended chapel. Sometimes the preaching was in Welsh and sometimes in Spanish, the number of Welsh speakers in the colony being currently estimated at 5,000. Next, the museum: here the lady in charge was chatting with a visitor – in Welsh, of course – so Billie took us round. On a map showing all the original plots of land along the Chubut River, she pointed out the smallholding that had belonged to her family. She was also able to comment, not always favourably, on the personalities of some of the worthies whose photographs hung round the walls: the struggle for survival, it seemed, sometimes became manifest in a certain harshness of character. Then she drove us round the *chacras* – the smallholdings – that surrounded Gaimán, with the apples in the orchards just ready for the picking. Farming here was still not all that easy: crops were often liable to be devastated by storms and floods. Much of the seasonal work was done by Indians from Bolivia, who were apparently more motivated than the locals. We also heard about the visit of Diana, Princess of Wales.

The Princess came to Argentina the year before her death, expressing a special wish to visit the Welsh colony. She wanted not only to view some of the spectacular wildlife to be found in the area, especially the whales off Puerto Madryn, but also to meet some of the people – and to visit one of the traditional *casas de té* in Gaimán. It is not difficult to imagine the speculation that went on. Which of the *casas* would have the honour of entertaining Lady Di? The oldest established, or the largest, or the one with the finest cuisine? In the end the answer was simple. It was the one with the most direct line to the official body in charge of the Princess's tour: a brand-new purpose-built establishment whose owner had not a drop of Welsh blood in his veins. One can imagine the quiet fury that prevailed. Just a storm in a teacup, perhaps – but the Welsh have long memories. Was this not why they came to Patagonia in the first place?

Our final visit was to the first house that had been built in the town, now just being restored as a historic monument: a surprisingly primitive structure. Then the bus for Trelew arrived, and we bade Billie an affectionate farewell. It had been a day of surprises – with one more yet to come.

That evening it took us a while to find a place to eat, and as we explored the town we became aware that something was going on. The streets were being cleared in preparation for some event, with barriers being set up across certain roads. As we were finishing our meal we heard the sound of drums. We followed the general direction of people and came out on the main street just as the first part of a procession was passing by. There was the band of drummers – mainly, it seemed, Indians – playing with enormous energy and intensity. They were following a troupe of scantily dressed girls – evidently locals since they came in all shapes and sizes – shimmying their way down the street. It made me feel quite chilly to see them, for there was already an autumnal nip in the air, but I suppose the energy being generated was enough to keep the cold at bay. After this lot, another band – some brass in this one as well as the drums – and another troupe of girls all in silver, led by the chief dancer, a tall and elegant black girl, the only one who really knew the steps. By the time the third band and its dancers were going by we began to realize what the celebration was all about. Carnival! Not just any old carnival, either – but carnival Rio-style. The samba schools of Rio de Janeiro, it seemed, had come south and were striking root in Patagonia.

Would these semi-naked girls, we wondered, be the same as those who sang angelically in the *eisteddfod* choirs, clad in traditional garb from head to toe? Or did this represent the opposition, challenged by the prevailing Celtic culture to assert its own identity?

But as we watched yet another posse of beauties boogie on down, Jeremy made the defining comment: 'Not exactly what the founding fathers had in mind!'

6. COMODORO

Now we were on our way to Comodoro Rivadavia, by long-distance double-decker bus. We left the large, well-organized Trelew terminal at 10 a.m., courtesy of the Don Otto bus company; we had booked well in advance and had seats right at the front, above the driver. Crossing the Chubut River and leaving behind the belt of poplars and green fields with grazing cows, we headed into the uninterrupted Patagonian pampa.

The land here was flat in every direction, with few distinguishing features. Patches of low-lying shrubs and bushes gave some variation but the main colour was a dusty brown, extending right to the horizon where it met the brilliant blue of the sky. Monotonous although the landscape was, there was still that exhilarating sense I remembered from childhood of being in the midst of enormous space, a sense of infinite potential. And something else I had forgotten until that moment was the quality of the light and the absolute clarity of the air.

As I looked down from my front seat I spotted a small creature, somewhat larger than a hedgehog, coming across the road. Instead of prickles it had a whitish, jointed shell which even, helmet-like, covered its dark, hairy head. It was an armadillo, which turned and scuttled back the way it came before it was run over. I had early memories of a sudden agitation in nearby bushes – 'Look, a piche!' – and perhaps the glimpse of an armour-plated tail vanishing from view. But this was the best sighting of the animal that I had ever had.

We settled into a comfortable stupor as the bus consumed the miles, halting at about midday for a welcome break at a garage-cum-snack-bar in the middle of nowhere. There was a cheerful family group near by enjoying an alfresco barbecue.

Around three in the afternoon the land began to crumple up into hills and valleys, still very bare and dry despite one or two patches of trees and greenness where the *estancias* – the farmsteads – were. Here and there, off to the right and left of us, we began to see the oil pumps: curious metal constructions dipping regularly up and down like large long-necked birds drinking. Then the road swooped dramatically down into Comodoro.

This still seemed, despite all the attempts to make it more pleasant, a raw oil town, although no doubt we should have found some redeeming features had we been staying for any length of time. As it was, our destination was Rada Tilly, the little seaside resort just along the coast. The taxi-driver we found to take us had never been there. He was full of complaints about the state of the economy. The oil boom of the past years, he explained, was now in decline, and times were getting harder. From time to time he took both hands off the wheel to emphasize this point. At Rada Tilly (now enormously expanded, he said) he enquired at the police station for directions to El Balcón, the hotel that Raquel had booked for us. We eventually found it, right at the other end of the bay, perched up high among a lot of unfinished buildings and unmade-up road.

No sooner had we got to our room than there was a phone call from Raquel. So when we were ready we walked across the sand of the bay, past the family groups still on holiday, and soon found her house on the sea front. Sitting on the seat outside was a large middle-aged man: Raquel's son whom I remembered as a three-year-old by the name of Robertito. Hugs and kisses, and then out came Raquel herself with tears in her eyes. Also there was Luisa (a cousin whom I just remembered) and the eldest daughter, called Raquel, too, whom I remembered as Trixie. We all trooped into the little old house and sat round a table, and they plied us with tea and handed round a large basket of cakes and pastries, as we began to catch up on everything.

I remembered, when I was about seven, accompanying my mother into San Julián on a visit to Raquel, then a slim, auburn-haired young woman with a soft, husky voice. Impatient with all the talking and anxious to get away, I ran out of the house and clambered into the car. A gust of wind slammed the door shut, trapping my finger in the hinge. It was not a serious injury, but it served to fix the event in my mind.

Now, at the age of seventy-eight, after years of teaching, Raquel's voice and figure had changed, but the red hair remained. Here was a person to whom one could relate instantly and who was evidently at the centre of a great circle of family, friends and people of all sorts. For fifty years Camila Raquel Aloyz de Simonato, to give her full name, had lived in Comodoro, as English teacher and head of the language department at one of the local colleges and later a founding member of the new military academy. People would wave to her as they drove past her house. 'I taught them all!' she said.

The two-roomed cabin, bought as a seaside holiday home, had once been the school house for the small local community. Here Raquel now lived all the year round, while the flat in Comodoro remained at the disposal of other members of the family. Oil paintings lined the walls, with an unfinished one still on the easel. Many were seascapes, portraits of the bay just outside the house in many different moods, but there were others, too: flower paintings, and some abstracts. Raquel's poetry, much of it in English, I knew about already, but the painting came as a surprise.

Photos were brought out. I recounted as best I could the lives of my brothers and sister and myself over the last half-century, an achievement not as difficult as it sounds given the attentiveness of the audience. Eventually the others left and we remained with Raquel, or Camila (her mother's name) as she now usually called herself.

We talked about my mother. Raquel had been educated at Northlands, one of the English boarding-schools in Buenos Aires, and Millicent, my mother, would invite her to the farm for a week or so each year during the long summer holidays. It would have made a welcome change from the small-town life of San Julián. Pottering round the large garden, helping to gather flowers and pick fruit, or sitting in on the lessons my mother was giving to the youngsters who lived on the farm settlement, were evidently important formative experiences for this intelligent girl.

'Her lessons were marvellous. They included everything: music, singing, languages, sewing, knitting, and, most important of all, she encouraged the children to observe and appreciate the flora and fauna of this country.' Raquel would not have known then that the teaching methods used by my mother, with their strong emphasis on practical activities, were some of the most advanced to be found anywhere at that time. They were based on the methods of Froebel, the great German pioneer in education whose work had been introduced into Britain by one of my great-grandfathers, William Henry Herford. They certainly worked well in this situation and may indeed have had some influence on Raquel when she began teaching herself.

Other skills were also passed on: 'I still practise the exercises your mother taught me – it's simple gym, but they keep me fit.'

What particularly impressed Raquel was my mother's interest in the natural world, particularly the indigenous plants and flowers. She had undertaken to collect, classify and paint as many of the local plants as possible and send the results of her research to the botanical department at Kew Gardens, since from the scientific point of view this was virgin territory. In doing this she was continuing the work begun by my grandmother, who had come out on a visit in 1909, and carried on by my Aunt Edith during what little spare time she had during the early years of the farm. What Raquel had never forgotten, however, was my mother's own creation: the bedspread on which she had traced and embroidered many of these flowers, revealing a love and enjoyment of the small plants that went far beyond purely scientific interest. One year, this was awarded first prize at the Exposición Rural in Buenos Aires.

Raquel then brought out a ceramic tile, set in wood and decorated with a striking design of cornflowers and harebells.

'Your mother gave me this,' she said. 'It means a great deal to me, and that's why I want to give it to you.'

'But if it's precious to you —' I said.

'*Because* it's precious to me. That's something my father taught me.'

After a while we went and sat outside on the seat, watching the light of the sunset reflected across the calm water of the bay. By now the families had all gone: the weekend was over and the summer almost at an end. We could understand why Raquel chose to live here, in season and out of season, and how she had been enabled to find her own inner peace in this place after a life that had had its share of turmoil and stress. This poem, which she had written the previous year, tells its own story.

Grey Dawn (1998)

Morn's coming
Sleep has flown —
My mind is troubled
By this grey dawn.

It rained last night,
Still clouds haven't gone,
Through the mist I hear
The roaring waves coming along.

The ceaseless struggle
Of the mighty sea
Rising and falling
Till eternity —

It's like unto
My restless soul
Soaring high,
Plunging low.

The old house is a
Lost ship at sea —

Surrounded by thick fogs
It gropes its way –
Coasting the beach,
A tireless phantom in the foam.

Life within me
Ebbs and flows,
Sinks with darkness
But rises with the dawn.

That night it rained, after a long period of drought.

We settled up at the hotel next morning and took ourselves off to Raquel's. The taxi-driver, realizing that we were British, wanted to know how people behaved towards us. Were they friendly? Yes, perfectly, we said. He was glad to hear it. There would be no problems with the ordinary people, he said; only the military might still be hostile.

It was a beautiful day. In Raquel's garden the almonds were ready for harvesting, and the dark grapes were ripe and heavy on the vine. She insisted on our picking a large bunch for our onward journey.

The dialogue continued: more stories from the past, while lunch was being prepared, cooked and eaten. The knowledge of the Aloyz family that I already possessed was confirmed and amplified. Raquel's parentage was typically Patagonian, her maternal grandmother being French and her grandfather a Yugoslav from the Dalmatian coast. They had lived originally in Buenos Aires, until rumours of gold in the extreme south of the country brought them down to Punta Arenas on the Straits of Magellan. The gold did not materialize in any significant quantity, and eventually the family moved up to San Julián.

The real name of Julio Aloyz, Raquel's father, was Yehuda Israel Yudelevich, and he was born in Tiraspol, a village in the Ukraine near Odessa. In 1903 came a pogrom – a massacre of the Jewish inhabitants – and some members of his family were shot, including his younger brother of twelve, a gifted violinist. In Odessa the statue of a young boy playing the violin is now a memorial to the sufferings of the Jewish people in that part of the world. Julio, aged fifteen, made his way to Odessa and boarded the first ship he could find – which happened to be going to the Chilean capital of Santiago where he had an uncle. Finding, however, that he did not get on with his uncle, he decided to seek his fortune down south. He journeyed through Chile and across to Argentina, sometimes living with Indians, and eventually got a job with an English company, peeling potatoes and waiting at table. His opportunity came when, one day, he caught sight of a set of accounts which his employers were discussing and was able to point out an error in the books. After this incident his fortunes began to turn. In due course he went to work for the San Julián Sheep Farming Company, and for many years the fortunes of our two families were interconnected.

The story of Julio's initiation at Coronel has passed into the common history of the farm. It seems that the young man, keen as mustard, presented himself for work on the first morning in immaculate riding gear. My uncle Robert was there to conduct him on a tour of some of the farm's land and to see how well he could manage a horse. In the course of the ride they came upon a shallow depression in the dust, in which there lay a clutch of enormous pale green eggs.

'What are these?' asked Julio.

'Ostrich eggs,' said my uncle.

'Are they good to eat?'

'Oh, yes! One of those would make a whole omelette.'

'Could I take one?'

'As many as you like!'

Julio wasted no time in leaping off his horse, collecting as many eggs as he could manage and stuffing them down the front of his jacket. My uncle watched without comment as Julio very carefully remounted his horse and continued the ride at a cautious pace. Then, without warning, Robert spurred his horse into a bumpy canter. Julio was obliged to follow suit, with disastrous results both for the eggs and for his brand new outfit. But he showed that he could take a joke and became a loyal friend of the family through bad times and good.

Raquel, with her cousin Luisa, came to stay on the farm when the second Aloyz baby was due. Raquel was eighteen at the time, and she recalled how my father, when the news of the birth was telephoned through, came out of the house ringing the school bell vigorously to notify the entire farm settlement of young Julito's safe arrival.

We heard about life in San Julián in the 1930s, when the sons and daughters of the first settlers – both the sheep farmers and those who lived in the port – began to grow up. It sounded quite a lively scene: 'There were parties, and dances that went on till seven in the morning – the Scotts, the Frazers, the Pattersons, your cousin Bob – all that crowd . . .'

Then came the Second World War. We recalled the names of some of the young Britons who had volunteered for active service; they included Bob Patterson, and Ronnie and Nora Frazer. Together they joined the contingent of British volunteers who were embarking from Buenos Aires on a ship whose name was well known to us both. She was called the *Avila Star*, and she never made it to Britain. Argentina was a neutral country until joining the Allies for the last three weeks of the war, and Buenos Aires was full of sympathizers on both sides. It would have been relatively simple to leak the time of the ship's departure, and out in the Atlantic the enemy torpedoes were waiting. The *Avila Star* was lost with all hands. In San Julián all who supported the cause of the Allies shared in the grieving.

Aged six, I went with my mother to visit the Frazer family on the neighbouring *estancia* of Colmena. I was sent to play in the garden while my mother sat on the terrace and talked with Mrs Frazer, who had lost two of her six children. I ran round the little gravel paths pretending to play and drawing closer and closer in fascination. I knew it was rude to stare – but I had never seen a grown-up cry before. She sat there helplessly, the tears running down her cheeks. My mother was trying to comfort her with earnest and gentle words, but it was quite clear to me that she was having precious little success.

Leaving the war behind and moving rapidly forward in time, we talked about a day in Comodoro in 1980, at the time of the annual agricultural show. Raquel, helping serve coffee at her *confiteria*, heard the sound of English conversation. Looking up, she caught sight of four young adults who looked remarkably familiar. 'You must be Blakes!' she exclaimed – and indeed they were. My niece and nephews – four of John's five children – had come up from Estancia Condor in the far south bringing with them a consignment of pedigree sheep: the Cormo Argentino, a new breed developed by my brother, which they were taking on tour round the agricultural show circuit of Patagonia. This was how, after many years, contact between the two families was restored.

We heard about Raquel's other two children – the daughter in Buenos Aires, the son in Milan, the four grandchildren all in Israel, and how Raquel herself travelled to Israel when her first great-grandchild was born. 'You can imagine what I felt going back to where Daddy's people came from!'

We also heard about Julio's other son, Luis – Raquel and Julito's half-brother whose mother had been a widow living in San Julián. For many years Luis had harboured a chip on his shoulder connected with his unofficial status, and for this reason Raquel had made a point of gathering him into the family circle. A recent photograph showed a striking likeness to his father – whereas Julito, the youngest of the family, took very definitely after Doña Camila.

After lunch, while Raquel was having a siesta, Jeremy and I took a stroll along the beach and back, noting the extraordinary variety of architecture that had sprung up along the sea front of Rada Tilly. It seemed that every kind of fantasy had been given material form: castles, chalets, even the perfect replica of a mosque. It was all a far cry from the original corrugated iron homesteads, the equivalent of the archetypal log cabin in this treeless land. We returned in time for tea and the arrival of the door-to-door minibus service that was to take us on the next leg of our journey. As we said goodbye to Raquel we felt the weight of her words: 'Friendship doesn't depend on time or distance.' We were not to see her again: she died the following year.

The other passengers on the nine-seater vehicle were a couple of about our age and a trio of younger people who were sharing a drink of *maté* – which replaces tea in Argentina – in a companionable sort of way. We fell into conversation with the couple, and I explained about my connection with San Julián. 'Arturo Blake's daughter?' exclaimed the husband. Naturally he knew all about the sale of the family farm, not to mention its present owner, and brought us up to date with other aspects of life in the port.

There was more scenic variety on this stretch of the journey. To begin with the highway ran alongside the sea and then, as we turned inland, we traversed several ranges of hills: a remote, primitive sort of landscape. Did these hills have names, I wondered, other than those bestowed on them by long-departed Indians? It was exactly the sort of terrain described by Raquel in another of her poems, written in English:

Patagonian Shadows

Walking alone through
Coarse grass and rugged bushes,
Climbing up
A wind-worn Patagonian hill.

I've seen the shadows -
The shadows of the smallest
Particle of sand,
The tiniest blade.

Heart-rending, windswept
Patagonian soil -
I've felt your shadows
Closing around, nailing me down
To this – your arid, beloved ground.

I was reminded of a conversation Raquel once had with her French grandmother.

'Now listen: you're going to school in the north. Will you promise me something?'

'What, Granny? You've told me that promises must be kept and never to make a promise if I don't know whether I can keep it.'

'You're learning! Well, promise me you'll come back here. Even if you don't earn a lot, even if it's a sacrifice, come back to Patagonia.'

So she had kept her promise.

Then the sun began to go down in a spectacular display of colour. This again was something I recalled from the early days: the dramatic quality of the cloudscapes. It had to do with the wide horizons and the clarity of the air – and also, quite simply, the fact that there was not a lot of competition from the land itself. Eventually it became dark and we were peering out at a sky full of stars but no recognizable constellations. Even if the Southern Cross had been visible I should not have been able to identify it.

Then there was a glow of light on the horizon. Was it the moon rising over the sea? No, it was a town. Don't get all excited, I told myself; it might be one of these subsidiary places – like Caleta Olivia – that I've never heard of. But no, the sign said Puerto San Julián, and within a few minutes we were driving down the wide street of this as yet unrecognizable town and checking in at a brand-new hyper-efficient hotel. Even though there might not be anyone to meet us, we had arrived.

7. SAN JULIÁN: BEGINNINGS

San Julián is one of Bruce Chatwin's 'three boring towns'. In lumping it together with Santa Cruz and Río Gallegos in this way, the famous travel writer made it clear that he had no interest whatsoever in sheep. Nevertheless, had it not been for the arrival of the flockmasters, San Julián would undoubtedly have just gone on being what it had been for centuries: a convenient natural harbour for passing vessels to shelter in.

Even in this capacity, though, it has its place in history. On the beach, well above the high-water line, there now stands a cross, complete with commemorative plaque. It establishes the fact that here in 1520 was celebrated the first mass in all the Americas. For this was where Magellan, on his voyage round the world, spent the winter – and had two of his sailors hanged for mutiny. Here, too, according to tradition, took place the encounter from which the entire region gets its name: the meeting with the local inhabitants, the nomadic Tehuelche Indians. The bulky appearance of their feet, bundled up in skins as a protection against the assortment of prickly, stinging and poisonous plants that make up most of the local vegetation, caused some wit among the astonished Spaniards to coin the word Patagón, or Big Foot. So what could be more natural than to call the entire region the Land of the Big-footed People?

It is recorded as well – in Italian, by the expedition's chronicler, Pigafetta – that Magellan captured one of the local Indians to take home as a prize. Like the Captain-General himself, however, the captive died in the Pacific – not at the hand of a Filipino warrior but of scurvy. How ironic that, on the very shores from which this Indian was taken, there still grows an insignificant plant with an odd, squiggly leaf and a pink, convolvulus-like flower that provides an antidote to this disease. In our childhood scurvy grass was as familiar to us as the daisy would be to someone born in Britain.

In 1578 came Sir Francis Drake, who re-enacted basically the same scenario, encamping for the winter and dealing summarily with insubordination. This time, however, there was only one mutineer, Thomas Doughty, beheaded for wanting to go back the way they had come – and the sea-captain did get round the world and home to tell the tale.

These events, it seems, were sufficient to put San Julián on the map, and all the early cartographers of the New World included the sheltered bay, since it was one of the very few places that could be identified with any certainty. Schouten and Lemaire's chart of 1615 puts it in red, as does Joao Teixera Albernoz in his twenty-two-chart survey of South America published in 1626. In 1633 J. de Laet of Amsterdam shows a river at San Julián, while a French map of 1683, by Sarre d'Abbéville, gives the river a name: Joannis Serrano. Pieter van der Aa, in 1715, goes so far as to show two rivers and, in proper Dutch style, calls the place Port San Juliaan.

Was there a river in those days? There is certainly not one now. Only the Indian women, according to Raquel's grandmother, said that once there had been a lake near Cabo Curioso to the north of the town. There is no sign of this today, and getting adequate supplies of water is a problem that still challenges the ingenuity of the local inhabitants.

During the next three centuries the Tehuelches continued to have the run of the land, no doubt watching with interest when from time to time a ship dropped anchor in the bay. In 1670 another Englishman, John Narborough, explored this part of the coast and his boatswain carved his own name, WOOD, in rock on the hill which is still called after him. In 1780 a group of Spaniards under Antonio de Viedma set up a colony a few miles inland, not far from an Indian encampment. Relations with local Indians were said to be friendly, but, in the absence of adequate support from Buenos Aires, the colonists were obliged to pull out four years later, and a few humps and bumps on a shingle ridge are now all that remain of La Florida Blanca.

Change began to creep up on the Indians in the nineteenth century. Ships made use of the sheltered harbour with increasing regularity. One of these was HMS *Beagle*, on her second voyage of exploration, with the young Charles Darwin on board.

January 9th, 1834 — Before it was dark the *Beagle* anchored in the fine spacious harbour of Port San Julián, situated about 110 miles to the south of Port Desire. We remained here eight days. The country is nearly similar to that of Port Desire, but, perhaps, rather more sterile. One day a party accompanied Captain FitzRoy on a long walk round the head of the harbour. We were eleven hours without tasting any water, and some of the party were quite exhausted. From the summit of a hill (since well-named Thirsty Hill) a fine lake was spied, and two of the party proceeded with concerted signals to show whether it was fresh water. What was our disappointment to find a snow-white expanse of salt, crystallized in great cubes! We attributed our extreme thirst to the dryness of the atmosphere; but whatever the cause might be, we were exceedingly glad late in the evening to get back to the boats.

The visit was not entirely fruitless, however, for to the south of the bay the party discovered a cache of prehistoric bones, which joined the vast collection of specimens packed into barrels and eventually shipped back to England.

I had no idea at the time, to what kind of animal these remains belonged. The puzzle, however, was soon solved when Mr Owen examined them; for he considers that they formed part of an animal allied to the guanaco or llama, but fully as large as the true camel. As all the existing members of the family of Camelidae are inhabitants of the most sterile countries, so may we suppose was this extinct kind.

But while Darwin was focusing his attention on the indigenous flora and fauna of the region, there were soon to be other visitors who were planning a significant addition to the local wildlife.

From the middle of the nineteenth century the government in Buenos Aires was aware that the great open spaces of southern Patagonia had considerable potential for development – and for conflict, for the danger of encroachment from the Chilean side was always present. But where were the settlers who could safeguard the territory for Argentina to come from? The climate and conditions could hardly be said to be attractive to immigrants from Mediterranean lands, people who were quite happy to make a go of it in the northern part of the country. Who in their right minds, though, would wish to settle in Patagonia?

There happened to be one ethnic group who did not seem to mind the hostile climate of the southern latitudes and who, having bagged a piece of disputed territory in the 1830s, seemed to be getting on with their lives there in a quite satisfactory way. These were the British sheep farmers in the Falkland Islands. Accordingly, the governor of the newly created southern territory of Santa Cruz, Carlos Moyano, acting on instructions from Buenos Aires, paid several visits to the islands and invited the British to come and settle in Patagonia, the land being available on very favourable terms. So successful were these visits, in fact, that Moyano went so far as to marry a Falkland Islander, a young woman by the name of Ethel Turner.

A number of farmers took up the offer of land. The fact was that by this time – the 1880s – sheep farming in the Falklands had become almost too successful. The Islands are not large, and the sheep population had increased so rapidly that there was a danger of overgrazing. One by one, farmers ventured across to the mainland and began to acquire tracts of land: Hallidays, Waldrons, Feltons and others whose names are still familiar on both sides of those South Atlantic waters. One of them was my grandfather.

Robert Blake was the third son of a prosperous Somerset family, descended collaterally from the Robert Blake who, in the seventeenth century, helped to command the Parliamentarian forces during the Civil War and ended up as Admiral of the Fleet. The Admiral never married. 'Not even his worst enemy', it was said, 'could associate his name with that of any woman.' Was this a comparison with a later holder of the title, Horatio Nelson? At any rate, the connection – descent from a first cousin – has always been a matter of some family pride. His latter-day namesake, however, was not only a married man but ended up with a family of eight children.

On leaving school the young Robert went to study engineering in Munich. It was an exciting time to be in Germany, for this was 1870 and the Franco-Prussian war was looming on the horizon. It seemed a natural thing, in such a time of crisis, to stand shoulder to shoulder with his student comrades and enlist in the German army, and he wrote home to inform his parents of his intention. They were horrified. They had just received a similar letter from Robert's elder brother Locke, currently studying in Paris, who was planning to join up and fight with the French. Both would-be soldiers received firm parental letters telling them to come straight home.

There still remained the problem of what to do with Robert, whose character seemed to demand an open-air, active life. A solution appeared from an unexpected quarter. His sister Emily had recently become engaged, and his prospective brother-in-law, Fred Cobb, had been appointed Colonial Manager in the newly established Falkland Islands Company. There were plenty of openings in the developing sheep-farming scene for an energetic young man, and at Fred Cobb's suggestion Robert decided to try his luck.

Arriving in the Falklands in 1873, he was soon invited by Ernest Holmested to join him in his new venture on West Falkland. In 1881 he brought to Hill Cove as his bride Dorothea, daughter of Unitarian minister and schoolmaster William Henry Herford. As Robert Blake's family grew, however, so did the need for funds. Enough money had to be generated from sheep farming to give the children a good education and for him to be able to return to his native Somerset and live the life of a country gentleman with his lady ('Dora must have her carriage and pair!'). By the end of the century the wool trade was booming, and this ambition was starting to become a reality. In 1898 the family was able to return to England and settle into a large house near South Petherton, and as the years went by the four boys went to Sedbergh, Dartmouth, Uppingham and Repton and the girls to Clifton High School and Roedean.

For my grandfather, the Patagonia enterprise was essentially a money-making concern, and his heart always remained at Hill Cove where most of his children had been born. But by the time he had made up his mind to the new venture most of the best land, lying on either side of the Magellan Straits, had already been taken. Two of his former shepherds, however, had gone prospecting further north and discovered that there was good sheep country near San Julián. With no capital of their own to set up the enterprise, they had written to him for help, and in 1891 he had sent over a shipload of ewes in the schooner *Rippling Wave*.

In 1892 he arrived at San Julián – at that time simply an anchorage for cargo ships with no facilities whatsoever – and visited the sheltered valley where the two shepherds, Munro and McCaskell, were living in a shanty beside a small stream. The place looked promising, although a constant watch had to be kept for marauding pumas; about forty of the big cats had been killed already. Blake agreed to go into partnership with the two men, and negotiations with a lawyer in Buenos Aires resulted in the initial leasing of 23,000 acres of land. On his return to England there followed a period of intensive planning and ordering of supplies of all kinds.

In February of the following year he sailed from the Falklands to Punta Arenas, Chile's most southerly port. Munro was there to meet him, with the news that the cargo ship *Cross Owen* had arrived from England, loaded with all the building materials for the new settlement. Blake felt a tingle of anticipation. He wrote to my grandmother: 'In some ways I feel a boy again [he was forty-three], i.e. the old feeling of having something to overcome, and a place to hammer in order, is on me; that feeling was more or less dead in the Falklands latterly, when everything was in order.'

San Julián, however, was five hundred miles away. With Munro and two others, riding and driving twenty-five horses, he set out early the next morning, travelling forty to fifty miles a day. 'We eat when we get the chance', he wrote to Dora, 'and drink anything that is wet. People do rough it out here. I don't think they work as hard as they do in the Falklands, but they have much more hardships to put up with.'

At last they caught sight of the range of flat-topped hills that surrounded San Julián. Climbing up on to the windswept pampa, they did not have far to go before reaching the valley where the new farm settlement lay. It was not much to look at. There were two small shanties and a cookhouse with only half a roof, stores lying around in the open and rubbish everywhere. Ten men were living and working here, seemingly unconcerned with the general state of disorder.

Blake's heart sank at the sight. Was this really worth the marathon journey? Had he made a big mistake in putting so much money into the place? But things started to look better after a good night's sleep, and he lost no time in 'hammering things into order'. Hearing the note of authority in his voice, the men jumped to it: the settlement was tidied up and a hole dug for rubbish — and more washing, it was said, was done in the next fortnight than in the whole of the past three months. But he ate with them in the cookhouse, knew how to share a joke and how to treat each man with respect.

The next task was to get the rest of the cargo unloaded from the *Cross Owen* which was still lying at anchor in Port San Julián, an hour and a half's ride from the settlement. Here piles of stores and materials had been dumped out on the open beach, while the stack of wool bales which was that year's wool clip sat waiting to be taken on board, under a dark and threatening sky. These were loaded up just in time before the first drops of rain began to fall, but there was a clear need for a storage shed on the beach.

By the end of the first week Blake was ready to see to his own accommodation. This consisted of a small wooden shed, six feet by nine, which had been made for him in sections by Sparrow's of Martock, not far from the family home in Somerset. This little hut was to be his home for the next six months as he organized the building of the settlement. In later years its size made it ideal for another purpose: it became a playhouse for subsequent generations of children living on the farm, providing a constant, tangible link with those early days.

At the end of March came the construction of San Julián's first building: a storehouse, thirty-five feet by fifteen, on the beach. Blake moved down to the port with a labourer and Ernest Behm the German carpenter; the latter was a 'clipper for work', wrote Blake. They finished the job in a week and were able to store all the rest of the cargo. Conditions were harsh and dusty; they sheltered under a bush at night, with a revolver to hand in case of attack by pumas, and at one stage they suffered severely from thirst.

After this the entire team sharpened their tools ready for the major task of building the shearing shed. This took five weeks, with Blake working alongside the others to ensure a high standard of workmanship. They were not completely isolated during this time; there were other passers-by, some of them driving flocks of sheep through to new settlements.

As the winter came on, however, these grew fewer in number and finally ceased altogether. In May it began to get colder and to freeze at night. With no heating in his small shanty, Blake found it impossible to read or write in the evenings, and after a short 'yarn' with the men he would huddle down in his bunk and try to keep warm under the guanaco-skin rug. It was a long, hard winter, enlivened only by a visit from Edward Mathews, manager of Port Howard in West Falkland, who had ridden up from Punta Arenas bringing a large packet of letters and all the latest news from the Falklands.

At last, in September, came the spring. Pumas became less common on the farm as they moved westwards with the warmer weather, following the guanaco and ostrich. Blake and the carpenter built two more shanties for shepherds in outlying parts of the farm. In November there was rain, bringing the small spring flowers: pink scurvy grass, Pale Maidens, yellow calceolarias, blue and purple vetches and pinky-white cactus flowers with petals like wax. Further afield the sweet-scented white blossom of the mata negra bushes and the brilliant scarlet of the gorse-like flame-bush added new tinges to the prevailing dun-coloured landscape. The sheep were in surprisingly good condition, and there were 5,000 lambs to be marked. The construction work had all been finished on schedule, and shearing started on the first day of November.

By this time supplies were running low; the tea and sugar were finished, and by the end of November the flour and soap had been used up, too. There was of course no shortage of mutton, and salt was always available from Darwin's nearby salt lagoon, but by now Blake felt that he never wanted to eat meat again. The shearing, however, had been completed, ending the first stage in the establishment of the new farm. Now it was possible to look forward to the time when he would be reunited with his family in England. But – sea travel being what it was in those days – it was not until the beginning of February 1894 that he eventually landed at Southampton, having been away from his family for nearly fifteen months.

8. EARLY DAYS AT CORONEL

For the next five years Donald Munro continued as farm manager, and it was during this period that Ned Chace, the 'Yankee in Patagonia', worked at Coronel as a carpenter. He left a pungent word-picture of his erstwhile boss, who was 'a little fellow with a big red beard and a stammer' but who, in Chace's opinion, knew more about sheep than any other man he had met in Patagonia. 'He was a funny little man with a cast in one eye . . . He wore a tam, a shabby coat with one sleeve out, never any buttons on his shirt, *bombachas* like the Indians and *alpargatas* . . . Munro looked worse than any of his *peóns* . . .' But according to John, a 'tame' Indian who had known Munro in Tierra del Fuego, 'he was a good man – he never hunted the Indians down, like other white men done. He only killed an Indian once, when an arrow went whizzin' by his head.'

Blake visited from time to time, acquiring more land when it became clear that this was indeed good sheep country. But in 1899 Munro died suddenly, leaving his financial affairs in a tangle. Blake had to embark in a hurry to sort matters out and to arrange for Robert Patterson from neighbouring Mata Grande to look after the farm for the time being.

By the turn of the century, however, Blake's eldest son, also called Robert, had decided to follow his father into sheep farming. After a number of years spent gaining experience in the Falklands, Australia, New Zealand and South Africa he arrived in San Julián in 1907 to take up his post as manager – quite an undertaking for a young man of twenty-three. He gave himself single-mindedly to the task, but it was a lonely and demanding job.

In 1911, however, he returned to the family home in Somerset to find that his sister Bridget had invited one of her old school friends to stay. A doctor's daughter, she was twenty-five, Scottish, small and bright-eyed, and her name was Edith Wedderburn. Her father had in 1900 attended the birth of the Lady Elizabeth Bowes-Lyon, later to become the Queen Mother.

The carefully laid plan was almost too successful. Robert fell head over heels in love with the newcomer and after a few days asked her to marry him. Edith, quite taken by surprise, refused. 'I hardly know you!' she said. Robert, completely shattered, took to his room. After a sleepless night,

Edith encountered him again the next evening and told him that she had changed her mind.

'Thank you, my dear,' said Robert, kissing her very gently. 'I hope you will never regret it.'

The newly wed couple arrived in San Julián on 27 September 1911 – Edith's birthday, as she recalled in her memoirs many years later. What in 1893 had been an empty beach was now a rough little seaport town of houses and shanties made of corrugated iron or rusty, flattened kerosene tins. In addition to the storage shed built by Robert's father there was a bank, a store and the small Hotel Miramar. Here they stayed overnight before driving out to Estancia Coronel, where Edith was to spend the next seventeen years of her life and where all but one of her children were born. But it was not easy being a woman in what was very much a man's world, particularly as her husband took his responsibilities so seriously.

'Edith was conscious', wrote her daughter Mary Trehearne, 'that she had lived through heroic times in bringing up a family of six in this remote part of Patagonia. She was cut off from friends and family for most of the time and had to endure a harsh, windy climate . . . Trees grew only in the garden under irrigation, but she was able to "make the desert blossom" through her hard work and loving care for the plants.'

At the same time, the Blakes in England were constantly aware of the young couple's need for support, and on more than one occasion, when Edith was feeling overwhelmed by the demands of family life, a team would be dispatched from home to help out. At various times both Blake parents, or one or other of Robert's three younger sisters, came to stay at Coronel. The eldest of the family, Elsie, had by this time emigrated to Canada for a pioneering life in Alberta. But, in a repetition of their own early life in the Falklands, Bridget, Violet and Dorothy (who eventually settled in Kenya) were ready to turn their hands to any practical task in Patagonia and always left Edith feeling cheered and strengthened.

In 1919 Robert's younger brother Arthur, then aged twenty-four, arrived to join the family firm. He had done war service with the Somerset Light Infantry in Mesopotamia, where he had been present at the capture of Basra in 1916 and had subsequently been awarded the OBE (Mil.). Besides shouldering some of Robert's burden of responsibility, Arthur was a great favourite with his young nieces and nephews, being always ready for a game or a romp. He played a key role, too, in a crisis that was shortly to hit the farm.

The Argentine government laid claim to the land on the basis of some alleged irregularity in the title deeds, and a notice of take-over was served.

On 12 February 1920 three men, accompanied by the local chief of police, arrived at the Casa Grande, demanding that Robert should hand over to them all documents and accounts. Then, since he refused to sign any papers, he was taken off to San Julián. Arthur, however, had been able to get there first and alert local friends, including the ever-loyal Julio Aloyz and a visiting lawyer from Gallegos.

Edith, with the four young children, the cook and the nursemaid, was left with the three men, who ordered the cook to prepare dinner and told Edith that they would require beds. Policemen were guarding the house back and front. Edith found the rifle that Robert always kept by him at night and took up a position on the stairs. 'If anyone sets foot on this stair,' she said, 'I'll fire!'

Confronted by this small, furious woman with a rifle, the men were taken aback and began to threaten, but nothing would move her from this position until Arthur, returned from the port, was allowed to sleep in the house.

Meanwhile, in San Julián, Robert was eventually allowed to spend the night in the house of Julio Aloyz, who was able to effect crucial liaison work with the lawyer whom Arthur had contacted earlier. Next day Robert was brought back to the farm, this time with the lawyer. Again he refused to sign anything. The family was obliged to pack and leave the farm, escorted by police cars. Next morning Robert was taken off to prison in Gallegos, leaving Arthur to look after Edith and the children. Edith was deeply appreciative of her young brother-in-law's support.

Robert was in jail for a month before the case came before the federal appeals court in La Plata, where the judge ruled in the Company's favour. After his release Edith and the family returned to England for the leave that was due to them, while Robert embarked on the labyrinthine legal process of repossessing the farm. It was not until early July that he disembarked in San Julián from Buenos Aires, bringing with him the judge from the neighbouring province of Chubut, to implement the decision. Julio Aloyz's house was again the base of operations. Arthur, Julio and their lawyer, who had all been monitoring the situation, were able to describe the incompetent way in which the Rodriguez brothers, the designated managers, had been running the farm. Their arguments persuaded the judge to conduct the rescue operation that very afternoon. With an escort of four armed police the party arrived at the main settlement, and this small show of force was sufficient to ensure a peaceful repossession, with both Rodriguez brothers being placed under detention.

'Robert . . . deputed Julio to represent him as host at the Port and stand drinks all round. This he did with gusto and in the course of the evening a large crowd collected for a celebration party at the Bank. Robert comments that no doubt Julio enjoyed it much more than he would have done himself.'

All that the ever-conscientious Robert wanted to do was to get on with setting the farm to rights. Five months of mismanagement had lost them 9,000 sheep, and it was going to take much longer than that before the farm could be restored to the state it had been in before what came to be known as the Intervention.

It was not until February 1921 that Robert, leaving Arthur in charge of the farm, was able to join Edith in England for a much-needed break. He could not relax for long, however, and after only three months was on his way back to Patagonia, leaving Edith, with the four children and the new baby Mary, to follow in November. It was while she and the family were still in Buenos Aires, waiting for the southbound steamer, that yet another crisis struck the farm.

There had been labour problems in Patagonia before. In 1914, for instance, the shearing on many of the farms in the San Julián area had been disrupted by strike action – but this time, in 1921, there was a much more serious uprising. The price of wool, driven up so high during the First World War by the constant demand for military uniforms, had by now subsided to a more normal level, with a corresponding effect on wages. The unrest spread from the south, with stories of armed groups of men taking over farms by force. Helped by Arthur's war experience and that of other ex-servicemen on the farm, Robert organized the defence of Estancia Coronel. He had good reason to do so. He wrote in a report to his father:

On Friday morning early, a band of men came to Colmena and took away all the men including Dot Frazer and Christian, the *capataz* [foreman] and a band of shearers from BA . . . A band also visited Salamanca, a little further south, and took away horses and motors and everybody except Andrew Kyle and his family . . . The two Mata Grande houses were burnt down on Sunday evening, woolshed and everything else being left untouched . . . A big crowd of men came to Cañadón Pardo on Monday at daylight, and took away as prisoners everyone except the boss, *capataz* and storekeeper, including a number of Scotsmen who were insufficiently armed. The telegraph line to the north is cut now . . . Shearing continues well but rather slowly . . .

December 2nd – Mulakaike, Bajo Picaso and Estancia Nuova have now all been visited by the bandits, all horses stolen, etc. The Machos shearers have all cleared out, frightened, so we are the only place near here working. Our shearers refused to work yesterday afternoon owing to some very exaggerated reports of the enemy's strength and brutality, which one cannot entirely prevent reaching the Settlement, but we have got them started again today. Julio came up from the Port yesterday and is stopping here at present. His tongue was an important and perhaps the chief factor in getting the shearers back to work again . . .

Our shepherds are all in the Settlement at present. Our neighbours on the south, west and north have been visited and robbed, but so far we have not had a telephone wire cut or a horse stolen, which is extraordinary. I am pretty sure they will not actually attack this Settlement: they don't like being shot at, but sheep farming under present conditions is not enjoyable.

It appeared that all the attacks on neighbouring farms had been inflicted by a gang of about twenty men armed with Winchesters and revolvers. These men were rounded up by government troops before Edith and her family left Buenos Aires. What became of them after that was no concern of the sheep-farming fraternity, but the evidence is that negotiation over wages did not play a major part in the government strategy of the time, and violence was met with violence.

From San Julián comes the story of the five girls from La Catalana, the local *casa de tolerancia*, who refused to have anything to do with a squad of soldiers just back from a campaign of extermination in the south, hunting down and killing a large number of strikers. The soldiers were furious at this rejection and tried to gatecrash an entry but were fended off by a hail of blows from brushes and broom handles.

'Murderers!' shrieked the women, one of them an English girl by the name of Maud Foster. 'We're not sleeping with murderers!' They were hauled up before a military tribunal for showing disrespect to the national uniform and siding with the strikers. In the event it was decided to hush the matter up, but the episode was later celebrated as a freelance protest against state brutality. It became known locally as the Revolt of the Catalanas – a reference to a well-known event in seventeenth-century Spanish history.

Edith and the children landed at San Julián on Christmas Day. 'But when Robert met them off the *chata* they could see that he was a very tired man . . . He and Arthur had borne most of the responsibility for defending the farm and looked drawn and haggard as if they had not slept properly for many nights.'

There was plenty to be done to settle the family back on the farm, but Edith's first priority was to get Robert to rest and unwind. When things had more or less returned to normal, it was Arthur's turn to go home on leave. He returned to Somerset to find that the home team, ever concerned for the well-being of its family members abroad, had once again been making plans.

One of the people they had invited to stay, together with her parents and younger brother Philip who had farming ambitions, was a young woman by the name of Millicent Worsley.

Millicent was born and brought up in the comfortable Birmingham suburb of Edgbaston. She could, on leaving boarding-school – Roedean – have gone to Cambridge, for she had gained a place at Newnham to read science. Instead, however, she began working for a social-science diploma at the Birmingham Settlement and learnt how the other half lived in that thriving industrial city.

'In the course of her training,' records the Old Girls section of the school magazine, 'she has to visit police courts, the prison and workhouses. Some of the homes are terrible, but she loves the work, especially that amongst children.'

To compensate for this, there was a lively social scene. It consisted of about forty young adults of her own age, all belonging to the prosperous Nonconformist families, either Quaker or Unitarian, who at that time formed the backbone of the Birmingham establishment and who were all more or less related to one another. It was all great fun, but sometimes Millicent hankered after a wider horizon than that offered by this agreeable suburban existence. So she welcomed the invitation to go and stay with these distant cousins in Somerset who had connections with South America.

Arriving at the large Blake family home, the Worsleys were given a warm welcome by their hosts, Cousin Robert and Cousin Dora, and all the younger Blakes. Confronted by so many new cousins at once, it was quite difficult to fit names to faces. Who, for example, was the charming old gentleman with white hair?

His name, it turned out, was Arthur, and he was not at all elderly: it was simply that his hair, by some genetic quirk, had gone white prematurely. Their engagement did not happen in quite such a dramatic fashion as Robert and Edith's, but when it was announced old Robert took Millicent aside.

'I think it would be a good idea if you stopped calling us "Cousin",' he said. 'From now on we can be "Granny" and "Granfy".'

Unlike the older couple, they opted for a longer engagement and agreed to get married on Arthur's next leave in two years' time, when Millicent would be twenty-three. That would give her time to prepare for her new life and acquire certain necessary skills: first aid, basic hairdressing – and how to tune a piano. Primary teaching methods were also going to be needed, and the practical experience acquired in the slums of Birmingham would certainly come in useful.

When she and Arthur arrived at Coronel in 1924 as man and wife, the place had become a settled community of several families, all English-speaking, with shepherds and *peóns* mainly speaking Spanish. Edith and her younger sister Midge had already established a teaching routine with the older children, and Millicent fitted in well, adding music to the curriculum. Later on, when Edith and Robert returned to England for good, she became responsible for all the teaching on the farm. In this she received a good deal of back-up from the family at home, particularly her sister-in-law Bridget who, a teacher herself, used to send out regular copies of *Child Education*, which was full of practical, innovative ideas. For four years, however, the two Blake families lived together on the farm: the Robert Blakes in the Casa Grande and Arthur and Millicent in the bungalow that had been built for them further up the valley.

She wrote for the 1926 Roedean school magazine:

We have been tremendously lucky in getting a three weeks' holiday at Christmas. We went right down to Punta Arenas in Chile, some 460 miles away, breaking the journey at various farms on the way. But it is absolutely impossible to make you understand the distances out here; you can travel for several hours across the pampa on the dead flat, and never see a rise in the ground or an undulation, even on the horizon. We crossed two rivers by driving the car on to a barge which was hauled over by men pulling on a fixed hawser. Our longest run in a day was 180 miles, and of course there were no roads, just two wheel ruts, and it was most awfully bumpy in places. Everyone was so good to us; all the managers of big places seemed to be British, and knew my father-in-law in the old pioneering days, or my brother-in-law. In Patagonia, nobody thinks anything of putting you up for the night on the spur of the moment . . . We also went a bit of the way up the west coast, seeing the foot of the really beautiful Cordilleras and just a glimpse of the Pacific. Christmas Day we spent out in the bush, our dinner consisting of a tin of sardines, a loaf of bread, a pineapple, a bottle of alleged port (sweet and brown and sticky) and two crackers, and we duly drank all the proper healths, sitting in the shelter of a prickly bush, on equally prickly grass!

At the beginning of 1928, the year of their departure, Edith was free to accompany Robert to the Deseado Show, the most important event in the sheep farmers' year in Santa Cruz Territory. Coronel sent six of its best pedigree Corriedale rams, and Edith and Robert arrived at the showground just in time to see their rams awarded both first and second prizes. Edith wrote to old Robert Blake, whose arthritis now confined him to a wheelchair: 'It seems such a good finish for Robert here – a crown to all his patient work and it does please me to see how much people think of his judgement and knowledge, besides the feeling that they are dealing with someone quite straight.'

Now it was the turn of my father to take over as manager, with my mother ready to play her part. By now the tough conditions of the early days had been replaced by a somewhat gentler lifestyle: the Big House was a gracious and homely place, and the garden that had been Edith's pride and joy was a source of pleasure to many visitors. 'The garden is my greatest regret in leaving this place,' she wrote; 'it has grown so wonderfully and every plant has its history.' Tobacco tins of plum and cherry stones sown by my grandfather in the early days; packets of seed sent through the post; cuttings of plants and shrubs from other *estancias*; currant bushes carefully nurtured – it was an inheritance fully appreciated by my mother.

One by one we appeared on the scene, two boys followed by two girls – myself the youngest – raised according to the same pattern: educated at home until old enough to be sent away to boarding-school in England. For, as my mother remarked in an interview to a local paper, the *Western Daily Press*, during one of the periods of home leave in the 1930s: 'We keep very British, though living in a foreign country.'

Meanwhile the young Robert Blakes were growing up in England. My grandfather, who died in 1931 at the age of eighty, probably hoped that his grandson of the same name, then aged fifteen, would also wish to make sheep farming his career. This turned out to be the case, and towards the end of the 1930s my cousin Bob returned to the farm where he had been born to begin the training that would equip him to succeed my father when his time came to retire from active management.

Everything changed, however, with the outbreak of the Second World War in September 1939. We returned to England early in 1940 for the home leave that was due to us, but after the fall of Dunkirk in May it was clear that we could not stay long. Rather than leave my two brothers at their English prep school, where they had been since the ages of seven and nine, my parents decided that we should all return together to Argentina, where we remained for the next seven years. The colonial-style pattern of shuttling to and from the mother country was now at an end, and we had to come to terms with the country in which we were actually living. My mother sat us all down and taught us Spanish one by one, so that we should speak correct Castilian and not just 'kitchen Spanish' – which we would have learnt anyway. My sister and I, when ready to go to secondary school, attended St Hilda's, one of the British-run schools in Buenos Aires, with lessons in Spanish in the mornings and English in the afternoons. My brothers crossed the Andes to the Grange School in Santiago, Chile, where a similar regime prevailed. By the time of our return to England in 1947 we were virtually bilingual, with an acceptance of a different culture that had not been present in the earlier generations of British settlers.

At the outbreak of war our cousin Bob, in common with many other young men and women of British extraction, volunteered to go and fight with the Allies. He trained in the Royal Air Force but never got into active service, for he was killed in a practice flight in 1941. It was now my father's task to find a successor in Argentina who would be capable of running the farm when the time came for him to take retirement.

9. IN SAN JULIÁN

It is 9 March 1999, 7 a.m. The sun is rising over the bay; our room faces the sea. It is a surprisingly windless day. Watched the wildfowl: a number of divers, and seven ducks flying low across the calm water. The place is *beautiful*, for heaven's sake!

As we were having breakfast I was summoned to the telephone.

'Rosemary, it's Cath. I was going to call round all the hotels till I found you. Get yourselves over here as soon as you can. Your room is waiting for you!'

We stood in the late summer sunshine waiting for the taxi; the border outside the hotel was bright with familiar garden flowers: roses, stocks, marigolds. A short ride – and there was Cath at the door of the house she now shared with Mary: smaller and white-haired now since the last time we had met in England but still, at eighty-one, a continuing link with the far-off days of my childhood. We all hugged one another: a real welcome home. Soon came a tap at the kitchen door – and who was this? It could only be Lidia, now aged seventy but still red-haired and lively, whom I was meeting again after a period of fifty-two years.

'How's Mary?' had to be one of my first questions.

'She's getting on all right now, but she's still convalescing in Sandy [Mann]'s house in Gallegos. It'll be a little while yet before she comes back up here.'

'Bessie kept us posted about everything that's been happening,' I explained. 'The last we heard, you had all gone down to Gallegos, and we didn't know if there would be anybody here at all. But we thought the only thing to do was just to get here, and take it from there.'

'We were very worried about her, but they seem to have caught the cancer in time. Now it's a question of how she gets on in the next few weeks.'

After that it was catching-up time again, and what our journey had been like – and photos, and how many children, and what they were all called . . .

'I was three years old,' said Cath once in a letter, 'when my parents left Lai Aike with the intention of returning to Scotland. When they got to San Julián, your uncle, Don Roberto, asked Father to take over for a few months while he was in England. The few months somehow stretched to more than half a century for the Mann family.'

Alec Mann became foreman at Coronel, and he and his wife Matilda went on to have eight more children, most of them born on the farm. Agnes, the youngest, was my contemporary. They were part of the community of families, English and Scottish, who grew up alongside us during the years between the wars. But while members of the Blake family came and went – to and from England, or to other parts of Argentina – the Mann family provided the continuity factor in the story of the farm at that time. Two of the Mann sisters, Mary and Lidia, had married the two Pickering brothers, Lionel and Tom, who were entrusted with the on-the-spot management of the farm under my father's direction after our return to England in 1947. When the farm was sold in 1978 both Pickering families retired to San Julián, and Mary and Lidia continued living there after the deaths of their respective husbands. Cath had pursued a teaching career both in England and in Montevideo. Bessie, the only member of the family to have settled in England, was an essential contact; it was she who had kept us up to date with the situation until the time of our departure for Argentina.

Now that we had touched base at last we were able to catch up on some of the homely things of life, such as getting washing done and arranging an appointment for Jeremy with the local dentist to repair the tooth damaged during the flight to Trelew. Cath apologized for booking him in under the name of Blake, but Jeremy was quite happy about this; as he pointed out, the name was not unknown in the town. I brought out the grapes from Raquel's garden in Comodoro, and Cath found a bowl to put them in.

After that we were free to set about the business of exploring San Julián. We set off down the wide central boulevard that led straight to the sea. How much of the town was I going to be able to recognize? My recollections of San Julián in the 1940s were of a dusty, one-horse sort of place with some 2,000 inhabitants. The single-storey houses were built mainly of corrugated iron – or even, on the outskirts, of flattened kerosene tins. A few wispy tamarisk trees here and there represented the sum total of the vegetation, for in those days there was little water to spare. Apart from whatever scanty rainwater might find its way into the roof cisterns, the only supply came by water-tanker, the *aguatero* driven by Nicanor Hernández. This plied backwards and forwards all day bringing water from the spring at Volonski's, the Ukrainian family who ran a smallholding on land rented from Coronel further up our valley. As children, one of our regular pastimes was to play 'Last Across' in front of the heavy *camión* as it lumbered along the road past the farm, churning the dusty track into ever deeper ruts. Arriving in the

Port, as Julito had recalled over our lunch in Buenos Aires, the *aguatero* would draw up, for example, at the Aloyz family house, and the small boy would be told, 'Go and tell your mother the *aguatero*'s here; she's at So-and-so's house.' Off he ran; but by the time he got to that house she had moved on to someone else's – and so on, round the town . . .

Then, in the 1940s, an engineer – a voluble Italian by the name of De Vita – was brought in to look for a water supply nearer at hand. His water divining apparatus, consisting of two flexible strips of dark whalebone bound together at one end, successfully located another spring on Coronel's land which was nearer to the Port, and San Julián at last had its own supply of piped water. While the well was being dug, as Cath and I reminded each other, De Vita's wife and daughter came out from the port to watch and decided after a while to go for a walk. They went over the hill into the next valley and got completely lost – an easy thing to do in that featureless terrain. Teams from the farm were sent out; they searched all night but it was not until the following morning that the two ladies turned up, scratched and weary, their stockings ripped to tatters but apparently none the worse for their adventure. Nowadays, so Cath told us, the town was supplied by a total of five wells, all on Coronel's land. But there still had to be careful regulation, with each half of the town receiving water on alternate days. Coronel, in return for providing the water, got free gas and electricity.

The population had by now increased fourfold to 8,000 inhabitants, and it soon became clear, as we walked round the town, what a difference the extra water had made. Trees, hedges and gardens now provided welcome visual refreshment. To the casual eye it might seem just another unremarkable suburban landscape, but for anyone knowing the old San Julián it represented a triumph. As for the shacks of corrugated iron there were still plenty of those to be seen. But interspersed as they were with a more respectable type of housing – brick or breeze-block faced with white plaster – they became buildings of character, picturesque rather than scruffy and worthy of conservation.

At last we reached the Plaza San Martín, the inevitable focus of every Argentine town. This, I remembered, was where we usually stopped and parked when we drove in from the farm. And there was the familiar bulk – so much smaller than I remembered it – of the Anónima, the department store where we did so much of our shopping. Sitting waiting in the car, I used to pick out the lettering along the side: *Soc. Imp. y Exp. de la Patagonia.* The lettering had long since gone, and the place was just an empty barn. A short walk down to the beach took us to the derelict jetty from which we had embarked on our last journey up the coast to Buenos Aires. A newer one, we noticed, had been built a hundred yards or so further along, but it did not look as if it were used very often. It was only to be expected. The shipping boom which had carried San Julián into the pages of the history books was now itself a part of history, and visiting ships were few and far between.

Another landmark we were unable to locate was the old Hotel Miramar, where we used to stay overnight when taking the early morning flight for Buenos Aires. It had always been an informal centre for the British community. Peter Bedetou the proprietor was very much a local character. The annual church service for the British community, for example, when the visiting padre – Anglican alternating with Church of Scotland – came travelling down the coast of Patagonia, was always held in the hotel dining-room, the tables pushed to the back, the pepper and salt cruets still gleaming on the white tablecloths. In earlier days, when Peter's wife, known as Mamita, acted as the local midwife, the place had sometimes become an impromptu hospital. But where was it now?

Don Julio's house, once the finest in the town, where we had many times received hospitality, was still there, overlooking the bay, but, as Raquel had warned us, in a sadly run-down state. We could not fail to notice, though, two or three brand-new groups of houses: handsome two-storey buildings standing head and shoulders above the others, one or two still in the process of being built. Someone, evidently, still believed that the place was worth investing in – but who? We added that question to the list we had already been compiling.

At this point it came on to rain, and it was time to return to base. Later in the afternoon Lidia arrived, proposing a drive round the town. She and Cath provided a running commentary as we travelled through the streets of memory. Yes, that was where the Hotel Miramar had stood; it had burnt down in 1968. Round the corner from the Anónima, and empty now, too, was the rather more ornate Argensud, the German-owned department store that Britons were not able to patronize during the Second World War. This was a source of regret for the British community, since it often stocked better-quality goods than the Anónima and items that were not easily obtainable anywhere else. This was one of the minor inconveniences of living in a neutral country during a major European war. It was awkward for the Germans, too, of course. There were no Nazis in San Julián, and the decent, law-abiding Teutonic citizens could at first see no reason why they should not continue to cooperate with their British neighbours. But war was war, and so the two communities had to agree not to be on speaking terms.

Next we came to the Sportsman café, which used to be the only place in town where you could get ice cream. Further along was the recreation ground, and opposite this stood the fancy façade of the Talía, the local cinema but now also advertising itself as a folk club. Lidia and I both recalled the great bazaars run there in the 1940s by the British community to raise funds for the Allied war effort. And then, round the corner, wonder of wonders, we came upon my favourite landmark, the House with the Eyebrows. The 'eyebrows' were ledges projecting over the two front windows, and whenever we drove through that part of town we sang out as we passed it, 'There's the house with the *eyebrows*!' And, although it was now a pastel green instead of the white that I remembered, it was indisputably the same building.

Recollections, of people as well as places, rose to the surface like bubbles; the songs my father used to make up:

> Oh, I went down south for to see the girls,
> Singing Polly-wolly-doodle all the day,
> For everyone says they are perfect pearls,
> Singing Polly-wolly-doodle all the day!
> Fare thee well, fare thee well, fare thee well my dear BA,
> For I'm off to Patagonnia because the girls are bonnier,
> Singing Polly-wolly-doodle all the day!
>
> Oh, the lovely dames of San Julián,
> Singing Polly-wolly-doodle all the day,
> They fairly captivate a man,
> Singing Polly-wolly-doodle all the day . . .

'Your father', said Lidia suddenly, 'was a very clever man. Much too clever to be a sheep farmer!' What did she mean by that? I wondered.

'Was Baum's shop here in your time?' I could not recall it. 'Anyway, you can get your postcards here.' We all piled into the stationery-cum-general store. Lidia introduced me to Señor Baum: 'Oh, yes,' he said, 'I remember your father.' And another bridge opened up into the past.

'Where would you like to go tomorrow?' asked Lidia at the end of our tour.

'I think I'd like to go out to Cabo Curioso,' I said.

'I shall be teaching, but I'm sure we can fix up something,' she said as she left.

Over supper and afterwards Cath continued to guide us through our exploration into times gone by. I wanted more information about the environmental disaster that had hit Patagonia in the early 1990s – a disaster that had gone virtually unreported in the world's media, although had it been anywhere else on the planet, I felt, it would have got some sort of a mention. But, as my brother in Gallegos remarked dryly at the time, 'It is not surprising that it did not get much into the world press, as it got little dice here. Oil-covered penguins off Peninsula Valdés got more column inches, and at least some attention from ecological bodies.'

On 13 August 1991 Mount Hudson, a volcano on the eastern face of the Andes that had been thought extinct, suddenly blew its top. Ashes and cinders rained down over the surrounding countryside for the next three or four days. But that was only the start of the catastrophe. The prevailing westerly winds carried the residual ash all the way across the continent to the Atlantic coast and beyond, even as far as the Falkland Islands. Some of it reached Buenos Aires in the north and Ushuaia in the south. In the Falklands, so I heard from my cousin Bill, the main effects were discerned in a dirtier than usual wool clip and sheep with their teeth ground down to the gums from chewing on the gritty vegetation. Over on the coast, however, it was a very different story.

'For two whole days the sky was completely dark,' Cath told us. 'Shepherds in outlying shanties really believed the end of the world had come.' The light, fine ash settled right across Patagonia, mainly in the area between San Julián and Deseado, in places up to a foot deep, and got into everything. The slightest breath of wind stirred it up into a choking fog. Many people had breathing difficulties; both Lidia and Lionel, for example, had to go to hospital in Gallegos. By the end of the year the ash had begun to disperse: in San Julián it eventually blew off into the sea – although there was one valley, Cath said, where it just blows round and round and never gets out – but the long-term problems had only just begun. These were all connected with the nature of the ash, which turned out, when analysed, to have a very high silicone content with therefore an exceptional capacity to absorb water. As my brother wrote in January 1992:

> Most of the area described had never recovered from the bad winter of 1985, which wiped out large numbers of sheep in poor order following on the drought of 1984 . . . The drama arises through the water situation: the hygroscopic silicates settle on waterholes, springs and any stream not big enough to carry it away and first form a sort of jelly or morass round the edges in which sheep get bogged and die. If wet, it no longer gets blown away by wind but the next wind gets more and so you get a build-up which may end by absorbing all the water . . . End of story – or at least end of possibility of running sheep.

Bessie in England had also written to me in Christmas 1991: 'It is the end of sheep farming in the area.' Indeed, for many local sheep farmers, who had

Casa Grande at Coronel, 1971

Left to right: Agnes Mann, Eleanor, Hugh and Rosemary Blake
at San Julián, 12 March 1947

Christ Church Cathedral, Port Stanley, 1992

Hill Cove, West Falkland

Pilgrims and philatelists outside the cathedral, Port Stanley, 23 February 1992

Archbishop Carey and the author at the races, Port Howard, 25 February 1992

Loading wool at San Julián in the 1930s

Raquel Aloyz de Simonato at Rada Tilly, March 1999

Robert Blake's warehouse, the first building in San Julián

The author with Lidia Pickering on the old tennis court at Coronel

View of Cerro Munro from Coronel

View of Estancia Coronel from Stony Hill, 1935

The author in Lapataia National Park with Lilián Burlando and
her grandson Tomás Fotheringham

Estancia Harberton with Thomas Goodall (centre, in dungarees)

Estancia Killik Aike Norte, Río Gallegos

Wool wagon at the centenary parade, San Julián, 2001

Puerto San Julián, 1971

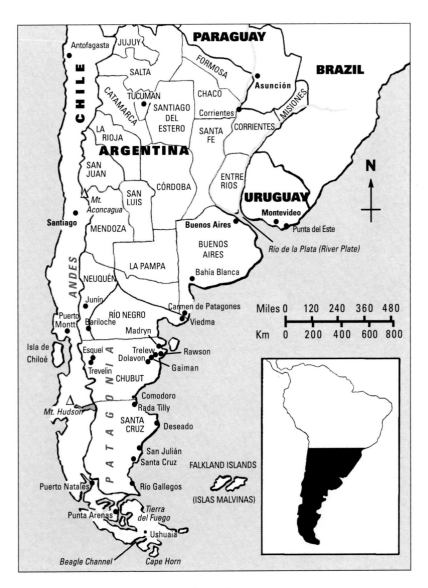

Argentina

Southern Patagonia

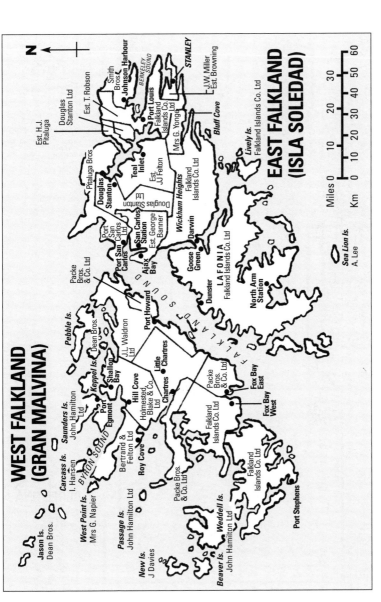

The Falkland Islands (Islas Malvinas)

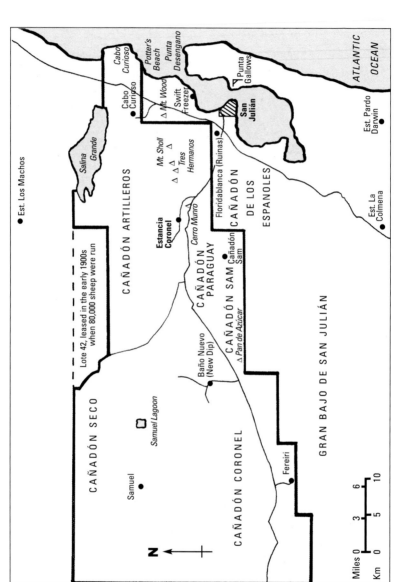

Estancia Coronel

been struggling to survive in the face of a number of natural disasters, not to mention a steady decline in the price of wool, it was the last straw. 'Gone are the years', Cath had written, 'when to say "*Es estanciero*" meant that if not rich, at least the owner was comfortably off. Now to say "He's a sheep farmer" is the same as saying "He's hanging on by his eyelashes."' For San Julián, whose development had been the simple result of the growth of sheep farming, the consequences were inevitable.

The signs of decline had been evident for some time before the Mount Hudson disaster. When John Pilkington, the 'Englishman in Patagonia', passed through in the late 1980s he noted:

> Like Santa Cruz the town seemed full of British pensioners. There was Lidia who devoted a whole day to driving me round and answering questions; Lionel who showed me the dried-up lake beds; Olive and Mary who fed me mountainous high teas; and Bessie and May, both well into their nineties, whose cottage had an outside lavatory, no running water, and a battle-scarred bust of Winston Churchill scowling from above the cast-iron stove. I could have spent weeks listening to stories from Model T days – but I still had a long way to go, and eventually bade farewell to the old-timers and set off north once more.

'The town', said Cath to us, 'was dying.'

But, we reflected, in spite of all the changes that had taken place, it did not look as if it were dying now. San Julián was still here and still ticking over. So what else had been going on during those years? We remembered what we had seen that morning and the question we were planning to ask.

'What about all those new houses?' we asked. 'Those fine two-storey estates?'

'Oh – well, that's the gold.'

Of course – the gold!

First from Julito in Buenos Aires, then from the Trelew taxi-driver – all the way down the coast, it seemed, we had been hearing stories about the gold. It had been discovered, we now learnt, some nine years previously, at an *estancia* by the name of La Vanguardia, a good many kilometres inland, and at first it was a closely guarded secret. It was now a government concern, run under extremely tight security, according to one of Mary's grandsons who worked in the San Julián office. The metals – gold and silver mixed together – were alluvial in origin and lying very near the surface. It was estimated that it would be about fifteen years before the deposits were worked out. Meanwhile there was work for those who needed it and some prosperity. So, for the present at least, the town had won a reprieve.

The following day was fine, with a light breeze; the absence of the usual Patagonian gale was notable. We spent the morning walking round with the camera. One building we were particularly pleased to record was the storage shed built by my grandfather, which had served as Julio Aloyz's office for a number of years. We noted with interest the newer buildings: the Catholic church with its ornamental spire and the German-built adult education institute. We tried to photograph the House with the Eyebrows, but the light was wrong; we would have to return in the evening.

Jeremy saw Eceiza, the dentist, first thing after lunch. A local boy, as we learnt from Cath, he seemed absurdly young, but inspired complete confidence. Since his brother was a dental technician it seemed that Jeremy's problem could be solved with the minimum of delay.

Lidia's car rolled up on time with a good-looking young man at the wheel: this was Mauricio, one of the grandsons. He spoke no English, so, with Cath as our guide, we juggled with the two languages as we headed north out of town. Our first stop was the *frigorífico*, the Swift's meat-packing plant – or rather the remains of it, for it had closed down years ago. In my childhood it was very much a part of the local scene, for 5,000 surplus sheep from Coronel were sent to it every year, and the manager and his wife, whether English or American, were always welcomed into the English-speaking community. From time to time we would be invited to visit, which could be something of a trial if the wind was blowing in the wrong direction. Long car rides tended to make me feel queasy anyway, and the powerful slaughterhouse smell that assailed us as we emerged from the car sometimes turned out to be the last straw as far as I was concerned. How, we always wondered, did you cope if you lived here all the time?

Today, however, the air blew clean and fresh as we got out and stood on the little headland overlooking the sea from where, as the rusty tackle still showed, the frozen carcasses used to be loaded on to the meat freighters and the residue from the slaughter discharged into the sea. It was Hugh, I think, who had provided the names for the place: there was the River of Blood, the Beach of Bones and the Bridge of Hanging Intestines. The River ran bright red as it cascaded continuously into the sea and fanned out into the surrounding blue-green; crowds of seagulls screeched and scavenged for the hearts and livers and lungs floating in the water. The place had a certain ghoulish fascination, but it was not somewhere you wanted to stay too long. Now just the occasional seagull drifted past and the sea below was a flawless blue. It was a peaceful spot to linger at and photograph the derelict buildings and machinery outlined dramatically against the cloud-dappled sky.

We then drove on, past the oddly shaped Cabo Curioso, into an area I had never been to before: magnificent wide vistas, blue blue sea, feathery clouds but all the land very dry. At the top of a cliff we got out to look at the sea-lion colony – unknown in our day – down on the beach below. There were not many animals left by this time of the year, but we were able to enjoy watching those that remained as they basked on the shore and occasionally took a swim out to sea. Meanwhile I was able to confirm my memory of some of the familiar plants: the clumps of stinging grass, the mounded prickly bush, the bright green poison bush – no change there . . . Then we returned to Cabo Curioso beach.

All this area had once been Company property. But because there was no road connecting it directly with the main settlement – although this was not a problem if you went on horseback – in order to get there we always had to go via San Julián. Sometimes we would visit the Kennedy family who lived there; Alec Kennedy had oversight of all that part of the camp. We were always given a warm welcome by Ethel Kennedy, whose two girls, Heather and Edith, were about the same age as Eleanor and myself. After the Second World War they all returned to Scotland and went into the bed-and-breakfast business, calling their house 'Patagonia'.

During the summer holidays our family would go out to Cabo Curioso beach for traditional seaside picnics, complete with buckets and spades. We had the wide sandy beach all to ourselves. As far as we were concerned, that was virtually the only thing that made it different from similar holidays in Britain – except that the beaches in Britain at the time were all barricaded with rolls of barbed wire. Nowadays, Cath told us, the place was very popular during the hot holiday period around Christmas, when parties of young people from San Julián would come out and camp near by. We took a short stroll along the shingle bank that lined the shore. The tide was in, and the place looked as familiar and unremarkable as any Sussex beach. It did not seem to fit in with my memory of the place, which included great overhanging sea-cliffs and miles and miles of sand. But then, I reflected later, my sense of relative space and distance would have changed considerably. As Cath remarked, 'You were a *little* girl then!'

We returned to San Julián to find that the light was in the right place to photograph the House with the Eyebrows. Mauricio, who had been somewhat reserved at the beginning of the trip, had quite thawed out by the time he dropped us at the house. Lidia told us later that he had a block about learning English because of the Malvinas war.

'He was only six at the time,' she said, 'and it all made such a big impression on him.'

A few months after our return to England, however, we had a letter from her in which she said: 'I have four of my grandsons now studying English with me. "Things are looking up!" as my father used to say.'

'There were black-out restrictions in San Julián during the Falklands war,' Cath told us. 'And they brought some of the troops down through here, young lads from Corrientes in the north. They didn't know where they were. "Is this the Malvinas?" they asked. They were all in thin uniforms; of course the climate was tropical where they came from!'

But, I reflected, leaving aside the slip-up over the uniforms – a serious enough error, as it turned out, since the campaign was fought in the autumn and it was getting colder by the day – it did make sense to recruit soldiers from the other end of the country. For there was always the risk that, had forces been recruited locally, some of the conscripts might have been in the position of having to attack their own kith and kin.

Although Gallegos was the main centre for air operations, San Julián provided a base for a squadron each of Daggers and Skyhawks, the rudimentary runway being reinforced with aluminium sheeting. Many families in the town invited the young conscripts into their homes for a good meal and a hot bath; most of them were further away from home than they had ever been in their lives. Meanwhile, over in Port Stanley, John Smith recorded similar instances of hospitality – unofficial in this case because strictly forbidden by the occupying authorities. Nobody could help feeling sorry for the youngsters.

At 8 p.m. Jeremy had a second appointment with the dentist, and again I acted as interpreter. The young man chatted away in a remarkably relaxed manner while he was drilling and was most interested to hear about my return to San Julián; he was familiar with some parts of Coronel and with the Volonski smallholding.

His style was very different from the formality of our dentist in the 1940s, whose name was Señor Lobo but who was very unwolf-like. He was fair, with crinkly hair and a neat moustache, and he had a young family. After the dentistry was over we would go with our mother into the *salón* for a chat with the *señora*. We would do the same if ever we went to see the doctor. This was all part of the conscious decision made by my parents to make friends with members of the local Argentine community and represented a shift away from the colonial-type attitudes of an earlier generation of Britons who preferred to remain as far as possible within their own national grouping.

It was late by the time we returned from our dental excursion, but in our absence Cath had been on the phone to the manager at Coronel: Leopoldo Henin, now in his mid-thirties, who had once been second in command under John at Condor.

'Leopoldo says there will be no problem about your going out to the farm tomorrow,' she said.

I could hardly believe what she was saying. Tomorrow, as it happened, was 11 March. It would be fifty-two years to the day since I had said goodbye to the farm, thinking I would never see it again.

10. BACK TO CORONEL

There had been some doubt, during the time that we were planning our trip, as to whether we would be able to visit Coronel at all. After its initial sale in 1978 to a meat trader by the name of Siracusa the farm was resold in 1996 to the corporate giant Benetton. The Italian-based firm had been buying up a number of redundant sheep farms in different parts of Patagonia, and the word was that company policy was very strict in the matter of allowing previous owners to revisit these properties. We had been quite prepared to receive the same treatment, but in San Julián it seemed that things were different. Our hostesses were on good terms with Coronel's present manager, who had said that we were welcome to visit whenever we wished.

We already had some idea of what to expect from Cath. 'You won't recognize the place,' she had written on hearing of our intention. 'The Casa Grande has disappeared, as have the rose bed and flower beds; it is all down to lawn. Many other landmarks have vanished, too, but what remains is beautifully kept, all the buildings painted and in good order.' This was in contrast, Cath said, with the state of the place under the farm's first buyer. 'We went out once, to find all the doors of the Casa Grande open, bales of hay in the *galería* [the glassed-in veranda], the house full of leaves and rubbish, lambs in the garden and turkeys strutting all over the place.' And Bessie had written simply: 'I was sorry that I had gone; we had such happy times there as children.' But Benetton, it seemed, had now taken things in hand.

I asked Cath, 'What about the old playhouse?' This was the small prefabricated hut brought out from England in which my grandfather had spent the winter of 1893 while the original settlement was being built and which later had been taken over by subsequent generations of children. In our day it stood next to the tennis court, surrounded by a child-sized wooden fence. A bird-box had been attached to the back; to my knowledge no birds ever nested there, but it came in handy if ever we were playing post offices. Before I left in 1947 I posted a letter to the children who might be playing there in the future. It was a cryptic compilation, full of jokes and puzzles, and I did not know whether I should have the nerve to look to see if it was still there.

'Yes, I thought you'd want to know about the hut,' she said. Then she explained that when Siracusa, the new buyer, was being shown over the farm, Mary had pointed out to him its historical significance. 'And he said, "*Sí, señora, eso lo respetaremos*" [We shall certainly respect that] . . . But then it was taken away and used as a shepherd's shanty somewhere out in camp. Mary never forgave him for that!'

Lidia arrived after breakfast, and it was clear that this morning was the best time to go out to the farm. So off we went, driving quite slowly along the shingled track, talking as we went about our life and family. The surrounding hills became more and more familiar. We reached the well-known point where the road forked right to the farm and the black-and-white wooden sign, painted by my mother, used to stand: *The San Julián Sheep Farming Co. – 5 km*. We stopped to take photographs of the new sign.

I was surprised at how quickly the conical shape of Cerro Munro loomed up on our left. But there was something odd about the summit. Traditionally, everyone who climbed the hill had to carry a stone to add to the cairn on the top – but this was something else. As we approached we were able to make out a rectangular shape with two shafts sticking out of it: it was none other than the old *chata*, the great wool wagon, crowning the summit, a landmark for all the countryside around.

Tom Pickering had put it there. Lidia described the planning her husband had put into the project, the team of horses struggling up the steep hillside, the downpour that nearly scuppered the whole enterprise. It seemed to me a flamboyant sort of gesture, a dramatic memorial to the end of an era.

Meanwhile, along there on our right was the familiar range of the Tres Hermanas hills – the Three Sisters – which it seemed as if I had only been seeing yesterday. Now we reached the location that had figured in so many of my dreams: the part of the track where the old road led off down towards the sea.

'That's something you won't have seen before,' said Lidia. We stared at the splashes of scarlet scattered across the valley bottom. Could it be the flame-bush? But that only bloomed in the spring. It turned out to be a great proliferation of wild rose bushes, bright with their autumnal harvest of rose hips. These had all sprung, so Cath told us later, from a single cutting brought out by Aunt Edith for Mary and Elizabeth's little garden by the playhouse.

'Your father always warned us about not letting them spread, as they wouldn't be good for the sheep,' said Lidia. 'Whenever he came to stay he would walk round and dig out as many as he could. But after it was sold I don't suppose anybody bothered.'

' "The desert shall blossom as the rose," ' quoted Jeremy.

Which sighting came first? Was it the old 'tuc-a-tuc' bush beside the track, home to the small burrowing rodents who used to call to each other in the guttural tones that gave them their name? Or was it the first building: the pedigree ram sheds down No. 5 paddock? Suddenly we were in the settlement: trees and more buildings, mostly painted, not very familiar – and the shearing shed, with a brand new addition that had just been put on. The green, meadow-like approach now seemed rather dry; the old *chata* that used to stand there was now, of course, on top of Cerro Munro. No horse corral, no chorus of barking dogs, a lot of buildings missing.

Up into the settlement, like driving into a village: neat, painted, tidy, along an unfamiliar avenue of poplars that had been planted in Lionel's time. Lidia could recognize Lionel and Mary's house and hers, but I was quite confused. We called in at one of the houses and met a nice young woman by the name of Dolores, the sub-manager's wife, who taught English in the port, but I still did not know where I was. Lidia parked the car a little further along and said, 'There's the tennis court.' We got out and, standing once more on the familiar concrete surface, I was at last able to orient myself.

All the same, it was a shock. The trees had grown so much – and yet everything looked much smaller now that I was grown to adult size. Inside me was a great welter of memories all struggling to get out. It seemed an impossible task to match up what was inside with what I was now seeing and experiencing. The only solution seemed to be to focus firmly on the here and now. I was glad to see a child's bike lying on the tennis court: so it was still being used as we had used it.

Although as we grew older we did occasionally play tennis, the concrete expanse was used much more for all kinds of other activities – for riding round and round on various pedal cars, bicycles, tricycles or roller skates; for playing different versions of 'He'; or for test-running oddly shaped vehicles made from assorted spare parts. In school time there would be organized games and gymnastics, led by my mother.

I only ever recall one real adult tennis party. That was a very special event: a send-off for those who were volunteering to join the armed services in the Second World War. Although I was only five or six at the time a mental snapshot of the occasion has always remained in my mind. Too young to play myself, I was, I think, supposed to be fielding stray tennis balls. At any rate I was off the court, watching the young adults at their game. A sea of blue flax flowers surrounded the rectangle of white concrete, varied at one end by orange splashes of Californian poppies and the dark green rice-grain leaves of creeping stone-crop.

'I'm roasting!' someone had shouted cheerfully. It was dark-haired, dark-eyed Ronnie Frazer. He stripped off his Fair Isle pullover and tossed it to the side of the court. A week later he and the other British volunteers were travelling up to Buenos Aires and embarking on the ill-fated *Avila Star*.

But the tennis court, once such a vast expanse, had now dwindled in size and significance. By contrast, the evergreen trees planted as windbreaks had grown out of all proportion. Dark and enormous, unclipped for years, they overshadowed everything. I looked across to the other side of the garden for further landmarks and found that the clump of willows was still there. Although they had evidently been cut back many times, they were still the same trees. There was of course no sign of the milking shed that used to stand just behind them. In the days before I went away to school I would get up at crack of dawn to watch the goats being milked, sometimes scooping a handful of nutty-flavoured bran out of the storage bin in the shed as I passed. There was no need now for the all-important fencing that used to protect the garden. Every so often the cry would go up, 'The goats have got in!' Then all available help was needed to get the omnivorous creatures out before they consumed vegetables, flowers and everything else within their reach.

The next thing that had to be confronted was the absence of the Big House which, even when empty, had presided benevolently over the settlement for so long. We walked towards where it had stood. There was nothing whatsoever to indicate that any building had ever been there, although Lidia and I between us were able to confirm its location.

The house had been built in 1909, along the lines of the Blake family home in the Falkland Islands, and was the only dwelling in the settlement to be built on two floors. It followed the usual construction of the time: timber framing clad with sheets of silver-grey corrugated iron and a red-painted corrugated iron roof. The rooms inside were lined with tongue-and-grooved deal boards or in some places with strawboard. The building did not have the solidity of a stone or brick construction and so responded freely to the movement of the air around it. When a gale was blowing the whole building creaked like a ship in a storm and draughts whistled through the rooms, sounding a different note according to the size of the aperture. Curled up in bed, you would have to block your ears against the shrill, insistent sound. Meanwhile the wind went roaring through the willows like a raging sea, and down in the settlement some twenty-five sheepdogs would suddenly raise their heads and start howling at the moon. When that was over the ducks outside the bedroom window, perhaps alarmed by a prowling skunk —

whose calling card could be smelt the next morning – would suddenly erupt in a chorus of frantic quacking. Nobody could have called it a quiet house.

A shallow flight of concrete steps led up to the front door that opened into the glassed-in porch, always bright with fuchsias and geraniums. These north-facing steps were a favourite sun-trap, and informal visitors would be invited to sit out there for pre-lunch drinks before going into the rather dark dining-room. I remember being part of a family group sitting on the steps in the sunshine with Lucas Bridges and his wife Jannette; their youngest son David was a contemporary of John's and went to the same boarding-school in Santiago. I found it hard to imagine this tall, urbane man, as he sipped his sherry and chatted with my father, spending his childhood and youth among the Indian tribes in the wilds of Tierra del Fuego.

Different parts of the house held different memories. I can recall the exact spot in the dining-room where I was standing when my elder sister Eleanor came in and said to me, in a curious sing-song voice, 'Bad news, bad news. Bob's dead.' Our good-looking, easy-going, popular cousin, heir apparent to the farm and so much a part of the family – no, I could not take it in. That moment remained suspended in time.

Across the hall, however, in the sitting-room, a later memory came to the surface. The war was over, and as we were relaxing one evening there came a tap on the window. Two smiling faces looked in: Mary Mann and Lionel Pickering. Lionel had been captured at Arnhem with the rest of his para-troop brigade and spent time as a prisoner of war. Now that he was back he and Mary were getting married – and he would eventually succeed my father as Coronel's manager. The future of the farm, for a time shrouded in uncertainty, had become clear once more.

The stairs leading to the six bedrooms on the floor above were next to the dining-room, with the bathroom facing you at the top. At that time – in the 1940s – the Casa Grande was the only house in the settlement with a flush toilet; everyone else had outdoor earth closets. The system, however, was not perfect, and one memorable year when we had another family – the Thorntons from Buenos Aires – staying with us, my father composed a little verse that was placed just above it:

> Lift and hold the handle tight,
> Till the pan is emptied quite.
> If you let it go too quick,
> The valve inside will simply stick.

And just above the wash basin was written:

When you wash your hands, you oughter
Clean them well with soap and water.
Remember it is very foul
To leave the dirt upon the towel.

To the right of the bathroom was our parents' bedroom, which we were allowed to invade on a Sunday morning when our father did not have to get up at crack of dawn. Here was the bedspread embroidered by my mother with all the small flowers of Patagonia – and here, too, in a drawer of the dressing-table, there lay, jet-black, heavy and sinister, a loaded revolver. There had never been any occasion to use it since the 1920s, but it was there just in case.

On the ground floor the passage to the right of the stairs led towards the back part of the house, with the pantry straight ahead and the kitchen door – which had its own distinctive shutting sound – on the left. The capacious kitchen itself, with the larder behind and quarters for a married couple behind that, was not territory that we ventured into very often. Only sometimes on a Monday morning, when all available hands were at work in the wash-house and it was my mother's task to see to the midday meal, were we children free to help or hinder in there, making dough-boys with currant eyes or later, under supervision, drop-scones on the kitchen range.

Behind the range was a space that came in useful at lambing time, where a young orphan or a rejected twin could be kept warm and raised on the bottle. One year during the Second World War a couple of ram lambs arrived and were patriotically christened Churchill and Roosevelt. Roosevelt, who had a fretful and persistent bleat, died quite early on, but Churchill grew and flourished. When he came to maturity he was entered for the San Julián show and won first prize in his class to everyone's great satisfaction. Another year there was a ewe lamb by the name of Elizabeth who became so attached to the household that she refused to leave the settlement altogether. Even when she was an adult with lambs of her own we might still meet her from time to time in one of the home paddocks.

The door on the right of the passage, facing the kitchen, led to the nursery, which was also the schoolroom and where we had meals if not everyone was at home. Here were the books, the toys and the elderly gramophone with a precious collection of records – and a canary in a cage who, for a while at least, coexisted with the cat. The window looked out on to the duck-pond and the drying-green, while the door on the north side led into the *galería*. This was the conservatory that provided vital space for us children during the colder seasons of the year and which could also serve as an extra classroom. One of my earliest recollections was of being pushed in a child's indoor swing slung from the ceiling – but indeed that room housed a great accumulation of memories. A door at the other end led down steps into the garden – another sun trap for summer days. On Christmas Day, when everyone in the settlement gathered in the garden at midday for the traditional *asado*, the *galería* sometimes became an impromptu dance hall for the remainder of the afternoon, courtesy of a portable wind-up gramophone. Outside, the summer sun beat down on the lawns and bright flower beds while those who did not feel like dancing sat and chatted or, in the case of the younger ones, played games.

Leaving the site of the house behind us, Lidia, Jeremy and I moved on up the garden. Here there had been apple trees and *guindas*, the sour dark-red morello cherries. Now there were no neat rows of vegetables, presided over by Lidia's father, Alec Mann, in his retirement. But then we found the line of concrete terracing, with steps at intervals, leading up the garden – a special path for us children to balance on – and there at the top still stood the row of fir trees, on guard like sentinels. Unkempt and overgrown although it all was, this patch of garden held a wonderful sense of peace.

Then we turned left, past the site of 'Schaer's house'. This house had been built for our parents when they were first married and was later occupied by Schaer, the German gardener. He had been a colonel in the German army in the First World War and so, with the outbreak of the Second World War, regrettably he had to be dismissed. The house then remained empty until it was eventually pulled down. We pushed our way through the tangle of weeds and unpruned trees – and there, just before we came out on to the track, was the octagonal water-tank, the scene of a memorable adventure involving a raft made out of empty oil-drums when three of us got very wet.

On the other side of the track there used to be a small graveyard enclosure with wooden crosses; Lidia and I spent some time searching for it among the dark clumps of *mata negra* bushes, but it was not to be found. Instead we took the higher of the two tracks that led up the valley towards No. 6 paddock and the ram sheds where the young lambs were kept, with the long-derelict Russians' Gardens beyond. A flint spearhead had once been found on this part of the track, a memento of the not-so-distant past when Indians had camped and hunted here. I always used to keep a careful eye on the ground whenever we came this way just in case there was another one.

Across the valley loomed the steep slope of the Stoney Hill, so hard for short legs to climb, so easy to run down. It was when you got to the top that you were most likely to find the deposits of prehistoric oyster shells which, when ground up, provided useful extra calcium for the hens. Along with the smooth sea-worn pebbles, they were the ultimate proof that all of this terrain had once been under the sea.

We had not gone very far up the valley, however, before we saw signs of activity; work of some sort was going on with a lorry. We were only visitors, after all, and had no right to intrude; it was time to turn back.

We worked our way down on the other side. The row of fir trees at the bottom of the garden had gone; now it was all green space down as far as the shearing shed. New fruit trees had been planted – apples and pears – and were bearing fine crops. Part of the pigsties could still be seen, but the dog kennels had vanished completely. Nor was there any sign of the horse corral, the stockade of stout posts that used to stand planted firmly in the midst of the settlement.

Perched on the row of kennels that backed on to the corral, we children were able to enjoy a grandstand view whenever there was work going on with the horses. Some of these might well have been descended from the troop of twenty-five animals driven up from Punta Arenas on my grandfather's marathon ride of 1893. While waiting for the show to start we would bang our heels against the backs of the corrugated-iron kennels to make the dogs bark. The horses, only half broken in, would be driven into the enclosure and made to trot round in a clockwise direction, which they did not always want to do. Then one of the shepherds, lasso in hand, would single out one of the herd and, whirling the rope round his head, let fly with the noose. Sometimes he was successful first time; sometimes it took several tries to get the noose over the animal's head. Then the rest of the rope was hitched round the post in the centre of the corral to take the strain as the horse, realizing it was caught, tried to pull away. The noose tightened until the animal had difficulty in breathing and its breath came loud and harsh. Gradually it was brought under control and, if branding was the order of the day, it would be taken to the side of the corral and made to lie down while a red-hot branding iron with the letter 'S' was quickly applied to its flank.

At other times the mares would be brought in with their foals when the youngsters were ready to be separated from their mothers. Or there would be breaking-in sessions when young horses were being mounted for the first time and would sometimes start bucking in true Western bronco style; these were the most exciting times of all. A good supply of horses was an essential resource. Each shepherd had to have two or three horses, for such were the distances that an animal could not work two days consecutively. The same applied to the dogs, which was why there were always so many of them in the settlement. We younger ones never ventured down there without a stick in our hand, for you could never tell which ones were friendly and which were not and might come up and give you a nip on the sly.

There did not seem to be any animals around at all now, until we got as far as the shearing-shed. Then we caught sight of a handful of sheep in one of the corrals behind the shed: a few stragglers, perhaps, that had been missed out when the main gathering took place, for shearing time was well over by now. Along the front side of the shed all the pens that used to hold the naked shorn sheep as they came out through the trap doors had been cleared away, and the old engine-room had gone. This was the heart-beat of the farm at shearing time, when its *chunk, chunk, ka-chunk, chunk* resounded all the way up the valley – it was strange to see it no longer there.

We ventured inside the large new annexe – built for what purpose it was not clear – where Lidia greeted a man she knew. Here we learnt more about Benetton's recent activities in the locality: how they had bought Lai Aike and had tried without success to buy both Darwin and Colmena. The deal with Los Machos had also fallen through. It was thought that a new law concerning the right to exploit any minerals found on the land might explain the company's desire to acquire more property in Patagonia, but for the present this was no more than speculation.

Inside the shearing shed proper we could see that a single row of mechanical shears still ran down one side. This, evidently, was all that was required these days, for Coronel was no longer a farm of 550 square miles, running 60,000 Corriedale sheep. As my aunt Edith wrote in 1911:

It was a great sight seeing a mob of several thousand sheep arriving – stringing down the track with the tired shepherds behind – they had usually started in the dark about 3 a.m. as they hoped to arrive before midday and the hot sun. They encouraged the sheep with shouts, rattling of tins with stones in them or bits of sacking used as a flail. Each shepherd had at least three dogs – you could work one in Spanish, one in English and one on the whistle as they had their own characteristics, some working wide on the fringes of the mob, others snapping at the heels of the flock to make them keep up. But by the time they reached the settlement men, dogs, horses and sheep were all exhausted. Sometimes they had done more than one day on the track from distant camps. The shepherds had the rest of the day off to rest and clean up and the dogs had to be fed. Towards evening the shed had to be filled for the shearing next day. They turned to at 6 a.m. when the sun appeared over the hill to make it warmer . . . Next day the shepherds had to start out again – before daylight.

Going further back to 1902, my grandfather, with young Robert, was working in this same shed – which he had helped to build with his own hands – sorting and classing the wool, one each side of the wool table. He wrote to my grandmother:

You can't think, or perhaps you can, how thoroughly I am enjoying the shed work, of course everybody gets tired in a shed after a long day, but I am always as fresh as possible in the morning. I love to hear the noise of the sheep and get a taste of all the old smells and the music of the shears and the push and hurry to keep the tables clear of wool when the fleeces are coming off fast; it's just splendid, and then the joy of being properly tired and being always ravenous when mealtimes come round. Then the packing of the wagons and to see the lumbering bullocks go off with their load . . . Then there is such variety in the men, such different types, I believe I have counted 14 different nationalities.

Shearing time in the 1940s was not all that different from these earlier experiences. There were still large masses of sheep to be moved from A to B, into the shed and out of it again. As soon as we were old enough we, too, became involved in the process, the all-important harvest of the year. Reinforcements were always welcome in the corrals to keep a steady supply of sheep moving into the holding pens inside the shed. 'Hup, hup, hup,' everyone shouted, to keep the creatures on the trot. It was hot, sweaty, dusty work, and by the end of a morning people's faces would be coated with dust like so many chimney sweeps.

The shed meanwhile was throbbing with activity. Beside each shearer lay one or two sheep with three legs tied together, ready for the moment when, with the man's feet planted on each side of the animal, the clippers would sweep down the length of its body to reveal the creamy inner fleece. A boy would be on hand to gather it up as it was cast on the floor and take it to the slatted wool tables in the centre of the shed where it was spread out, the dirty bits were pulled off and it was rolled skilfully into a tight bundle. A job I particularly enjoyed was helping to move these animal-smelling bundles up to the quieter end of the shed to fill the two great wooden containers of the hydraulic press which was worked by our friends Morales and Panayote, the Greek from Crete. From here, by a process that never ceased to fascinate me, emerged the ton-weight, sacking-clad bales bound with strips of metal, ready to be loaded on to the waiting *camión* and carried off to the port.

In the middle of the afternoon the cook would arrive, carrying a vast kettle and a mass of tin mugs all strung by the handle on a piece of wire, and everyone stopped for a break. Whether in the form of tea, coffee or bitter *maté*, the sweating shearers were thankful for the lifesaving liquid. Meanwhile the engine thumped on, and the incessant bleating of the sheep resounded all the way up the valley.

Today the shed was silent, but there was still the same residual smell. One of the wool press containers was sitting by itself on the floor, looking as if it had not been used for years. There were a few bales around and some loose fleeces; that was all.

Outside once more, we had a quick look at the long, narrow trough of the dip. The animals would be flung in at one end and then had to struggle through the pungent-smelling liquid to emerge, dark yellow in colour, on to the dripping stage. The dip did not look as if it had been much in use recently. Other methods such as spraying were now being used to control scab, the bane of the sheep farmer's life.

We moved on down to the pedigree ram sheds which nowadays, it seemed from the harness hung up inside, were in use as stables. I recalled the handsome pampered animals that had been kept here, with as much fodder as they wanted and a large block of pink rock salt for them to lick. This was the prestige department: from here potential champions would be transported to the great agricultural shows, often to return with brightly coloured rosettes pinned to their head harnesses and another silver cup to add to the display in the dining-room. The years 1936, 1939 and 1940 were when Coronel took the top awards at the national Palermo showground in Buenos Aires. If pedigree stock was being bred on the *estancia* now, the animals were not kept here.

By this time Jeremy had run out of film and the morning was well advanced. Lidia offered to bring us out again in the afternoon to climb part way up Cerro Munro and photograph the farm from there. My mother had once done a watercolour painting of it from that point, and I had promised my brother Hugh to bring him back a snapshot of the same view. So off we went back to San Julián, where Cath had lunch waiting for us.

After lunch there was one last visit to the dentist to be made. We had to wait so long that by the time we came out it was time to go to Lidia's for tea. In any case her car had gone on strike, so it was not possible to return to Coronel as we had planned. I reflected that perhaps, after such an intensive experience, it was just as well.

Gathered round the tea table – a real traditional farmhouse spread – were Lidia's recently widowed daughter Susan, with her twin sister Carol and the latter's little boy. Both twins had their father Tom's bright blue eyes. Susan's three sons also looked in: Mauricio, Rubén and Darío. The latter had children of his own, so that Lidia was already a great-grandmother. All of Lidia's five children had grown up at Coronel, as had Mary's four. At one stage during this period there were seventeen children living there and the Casa Grande was in use as a school, with a professional teacher in residence – but by this time the teaching was all being done in Spanish. A number of this younger generation spoke no English at all or spoke it as a foreign language, in spite of being entirely British in origin. Spanish was now their mother tongue.

'I thought you might be interested to see this,' said Lidia. I looked at the typewritten sheet she handed me. 'It's about Tilly.'

Tilly, dark and attractive and next in age to Lidia, had never married but had had a successful career as a teacher in Buenos Aires. After her untimely death from lung cancer in 1994 – 'She always loved a smoke,' said Lidia – her school dedicated a classroom to her memory. I read the citation, which described the sparkle, the humour, the spirit she brought to her work. My mother, I thought, would have been so pleased. Indeed, I reflected further, she would have been proud of the way all her old pupils had turned out – not just in terms of academic or worldly achievement but in terms of character and the way they had dealt with adversity when it came into their lives.

After tea Lidia took us round to call on Raquel's cousin Nene Giuvetich, but she was not at home. We strolled slowly back to Cath's, and by the time we got there I had just about caught up on all the remaining members of the Mann family.

'I've been talking with Mary in Gallegos,' said Cath on our return, 'and she's obviously a lot better. She told me off for not getting you to visit the Ceramic Museum!'

This being our last night in San Julián, we invited Cath and Lidia out for a meal. It was the least we could do to show our appreciation. Thanks to their unstinting hospitality I had been able to get reconnected with the distant days of my childhood.

11. RÍO GALLEGOS

It was 12 March. Fifty-two years ago today I had sailed out of the port of San Julián with my family, *en route* for Buenos Aires and for England – as I thought, for ever.

Jeremy and I were up at 5 a.m., to be collected at 6 a.m. by the other door-to-door minibus. At breakfast Cath told us about San Julián's further mineral resources: the kaolin and the great deposits of china clay. We were all set to devise a scheme for developing a full-blown ceramic industry when the minibus arrived. There was time for one last hug before we hit the road.

The northbound minibus service running between San Julián and Comodoro, so we had learnt from Cath, was started by Dottie (aka David) Frazer after his small farm had been wiped out by the Hudson volcano. We were now, however, heading south to Río Gallegos on Daniel Ponce's minibus, a journey of some four hours. I had never before been further south than San Julián.

I fell into conversation with my neighbour who, like most other local people, was familiar with Coronel and its story; she also remarked upon Lidia's gift for teaching English. I asked her about her experience of the volcano. The worst thing about it, she said, was the dust that got absolutely everywhere; it was impossible to keep anything clean. On the other hand, if you were wiping it off a polished surface you ended up with a beautiful shine. That was the silicone, of course.

The sun was up by the time we got to the Santa Cruz River. My father's words sprang to mind:

> Oh, the lovely girls of Santa Cruz,
> Singing Polly-wolly-doodle all the day,
> I lost my heart, and with good excuse -
> Singing Polly-wolly-doodle all the day!
> Fare thee well, fare thee well, fare thee well, my dear BA,
> For I'm off to Patagonnia because the girls are bonnier,
> Singing Polly-wolly-doodle all the day!

'Wandering the streets of Santa Cruz,' wrote John Pilkington, 'I got the impression that it had always been a home to stubborn old ladies.' Might these, in their youth, have been the ones that had captivated my father over fifty years ago?

> At last I came to Gallegos town,
> Singing Polly-wolly-doodle all the day,
> I married a peach, and settled down,
> Singing Polly-wolly-doodle all the day!

Shortly before ten o'clock we came through a break in the hills and could see ahead of us the wide reaches of the Gallegos River, with the town spread out along its southern bank. Clearly this place was in a different league from San Julián. In addition to being a centre for the major sheep farms in the area, it was an oil town and a military air base: it was from here that most of the Argentine air-force pilots had taken off in their sorties over the Falkland Islands. Soon we were crossing the river and, heading into the town centre, were deposited on the steps of the small hotel where we were booked to spend that night.

We found Gallegos to be a pleasant, bustling sort of place, with all the amenities of a prosperous country town. We lost no time in making two essential phone calls: one to my sister-in-law Monica and one to the house of Cath's and Lidia's brother Sandy. Mary Pickering was still convalescing there after her operation, and we hoped that she would be well enough to see us.

'She'll certainly want to see you!' said Sandy's wife Dorothy. 'You'll come to tea, won't you?' So that was that.

A short walk from the centre brought us to Keokén, John's and Monica's town house that doubled as a shop for my sister-in-law's handicraft business. Monica was there to welcome us; she was staying for a few days in Gallegos while John was up in Buenos Aires attending the reception for the Prince of Wales.

The theme of the craft shop was wool – wool in every conceivable shape and form. From large, handsome chunky sweaters down to the smallest knitted toy, the qualities of the fleece were deployed in all their variety. Hanks of natural yarn occupied any space not taken up by the finished products, inviting the customer to get involved in some personal creativity. The undyed wool was of a remarkable whiteness – or so it seemed to me, recalling the off-white of our Corriedale fleeces at Coronel. But then this wool was different; it came from the new breed developed by my brother, the Cormo Argentino, in which elements of both Corriedale and Merino breeds had been combined.

Monica's involvement in the craft business had developed gradually over the years. First of all there was the knitting machine, which had enabled her to make most of the sweaters and cardigans for her growing family of five children. After that came the local bazaars which were raising funds for projects within the British community. From being a producer herself she developed into an organizer, mobilizing the talents of local craftswomen. It then became clear that there was an ongoing demand for all these handmade products, and it was at this point that Monica, with her friend Florita Lofredo, set up Keokén, the craft shop. This enabled many women to supplement their existing income in a practical way, while making a useful contribution to the budding tourist industry.

Monica took us for a stroll down to the sea front, an extensive area providing an appropriate setting for national monuments of various kinds. These included a centenary stone recording the early settlers in Santa Cruz province with our grandfather's name on it and another commemorating the pilots who died in the Falklands War. No sooner had we got back to the shop than a car raced down the street and pulled up sharply. Out of it sprang a large, familiar, rubicund figure who enveloped me in a great bear-hug and shook Jeremy warmly by the hand.

'Sandy!' said I. 'Long time no see!' We said goodbye to Monica, arranging to meet her for dinner at the British Club that evening and bundled into the car.

Sandy, Alec Mann's second son, had for many years been manager at Estancia Sara, on the northern part of Tierra del Fuego, and he still returned there frequently. At his house in the suburbs of Gallegos we had a warm welcome from his wife Dorothy (the sister of Lionel and Tom Pickering), from their eldest son George – who, I thought, bore a strong resemblance to his late Uncle Lionel – and from Mary's daughter Doreen. We sat round a tea table loaded with traditional home-made fare, talking and talking. We had our story to tell; they had theirs. Naturally they wanted to hear all about our impressions of Coronel, which was as much a part of their family history as it was of ours.

'I wouldn't like to go back there now,' said Dorothy. 'Not with the Casa Grande gone. Sandy and I were married there, you know. I remember coming down those stairs in my wedding dress . . .'

And I – I thought to myself – remembered falling down them, from top to bottom, at the age of five. And in February of 1920 my Aunt Edith stood at the top, shotgun in hand, defying the gang of men who had come to take over the farm. Now those stairs simply did not exist any more, yet here we all were with our memories, creating the place anew in our minds.

After tea we were able to look in to see Mary, who was in an adjacent room, convalescing after her emergency cancer operation. Still looking thin and tired as she lay in bed, she greeted us both lovingly.

Mary had been born at Coronel and, apart from three years of training as a nurse at the British Hospital in Montevideo, had spent all her life on the farm until it was sold in 1978. When the two tall, good-looking Pickering brothers from Deseado arrived at Coronel in 1942, it was not long before Lionel, the elder, became engaged to pretty Mary with her wavy hair. It soon became clear too that Mary's younger sister, red-haired Lidia, was getting on like a house on fire with Tom. But then Lionel decided to volunteer for war service in Europe and joined the Parachute Regiment. Mary joined the ranks of those watching and waiting for the safe return of their loved ones.

Several months later I was delighted to hear from my mother that Agnes, the youngest of the Mann family, who was then about eight and shared daily lessons with me, would be coming to spend a few nights with us in the Casa Grande. Mrs Mann, apparently, was not well, and needed a rest. During the course of lessons next morning my mother was suddenly called out of the room. When she came back, to my great surprise, she held out her arms to Agnes, who burst into tears and buried her head on my mother's shoulder. For Mrs Mann had died in the night, at the early age of forty-nine.

A day or two later my father came back to the house with a strange story. Willie, the eldest of the Mann brothers, had had a vivid dream in which he saw Lionel standing on a pile of wool bales, fighting for his life with a knife. Like the rest of the family Willie was of course very much upset by his mother's death – but was there more to it than that?

'Willie,' said my father, 'make a note of the date when you had that dream.' The news came through about a week later that Lionel had been captured at Arnhem – and the date of his capture was the date of Willie's dream.

Those anxious wartime years brought the two families close together, and the bond was maintained after our family returned to England. Every two or three years both my parents made regular visits to the farm, my father to advise on the management of the farm and my mother to provide similar support for the young wives with their growing families. Her sudden death of a stroke in 1964 was as much a loss to the families in Patagonia as to our family in England. For, as Bessie wrote to me at the time, 'Your mother had a good hand in moulding the lives of all the Mann family.'

For some years my father continued to travel out on his own. In a letter to me in his characteristic spiky handwriting while staying with John and his family at Condor in April 1967, he wrote: 'I left them all well at San Julián with no serious problems on hand . . . Lionel and Mary are both well, but there was evidence that their personal tragedy, now a year old, is still fairly close to the surface, and it is a good thing that they are going off on leave during July and August.'

The tragedy to which he was referring was the death of Adrian, eldest of Lionel's and Mary's children and their only son, at the age of nineteen. The young man had been studying agriculture in Buenos Aires, ready to follow his father into sheep farming, when he was taken ill. His mother was just able to get to see him before he died.

All these things were in my mind as we greeted Mary. I was concerned not to tire her, but she was glad to see us, for there were certain things she wanted to share with us. Her deeply ingrained sense of responsibility would not let her rest until she had dealt with one particular subject.

'The playhouse!' she said. 'It's been taken away . . .'

'I know,' I said. 'Cath told us; it's all right. It was wonderful just to see the farm again, anyway.'

Then we talked about the daughters and how they were all getting on. There was Elaine in Gallegos, celebrating her silver wedding; Muriel in Buenos Aires; and Doreen who ran a bakery in San Julián. That made me think of Mary's mother, who had taught my mother how to make scones and who baked fresh for her large family every day.

Half an hour was as much as we allowed ourselves in her company. When we returned to the living-room another surprise awaited us – and another big hug.

'Duncan!' I cried. Not that I would have recognized him as the carroty-haired boy next in age to Agnes, if he had not said who he was. He was there with his little granddaughter: a regular part of the Gallegos scene, where he ran a garage. Shortly afterwards there was another ring at the bell.

'Remember me?' said a voice. 'Naomi Kennard from St Hilda's? Naomi O'Byrne now – but I'm a widow.' One of her sons, Erroll, ran Estancia Cullen on Tierra del Fuego, having followed Leopoldo Henin as second manager at Condor, while the other son was currently in Ushuaia.

The gathering got more and more cheerful until the room was fairly humming with talk and laughter.

'Heavens!' I exclaimed. 'We've got to keep an eye on the time – but we must have some photos!' We piled out into the garden for a hilarious photo session, after which there was just time to look in and say goodbye to Mary. Her parting words were: 'We are all one family!'

Then Sandy whisked us back to our hotel in time for us to tidy up and get along to the British Club where Monica awaited us.

The British Club – now the only one in the whole of Argentina – had once been the main social centre for all the prosperous British sheep farmers in the district. With the decline of the wool industry, however, the establishment's insistence on Britishness had got rather diluted. Bruce Chatwin, visiting in the 1970s, recorded that he had not heard a word of English spoken there, although John Pilkington, invited to the Club's AGM some ten years later, had a different story to tell. 'Behind a mahogany bar, white-uniformed barmen were polishing glasses and serving malt whiskies to refresh the members after their journeys in from the farms. The men perched on barstools and called each other "Archie old boy" and "Oh, come on now, Henry."'

Nine years later the well-appointed dining-room, when we entered it with Monica, was empty except for an Argentine family party – but of course we were dining early by Hispanic standards. Monica told us more about those crowded festive gatherings of earlier years, when everyone would arrive with great dishes of home-cooked food and there was a lively atmosphere of enjoyment and jollification. This was during the good times of the 1960s when wool prices were still high despite increasing competition from the man-made fibre market that developed after the end of the Second World War. But by the time of John Pilkington's visit in 1990, as he learnt from one of the farmers, 'In this province, one farm in ten has already gone down.'

Monica, indeed, had seen many changes since she first joined the sheep-farming fraternity as a young bride. Her meeting with John was a classic shipboard romance. John was travelling out to Patagonia to spend a season at Coronel. After this he was due to become second in command at Hill Cove where he would be working under his cousin Bill, Uncle Robert's second son. Following the death of his elder brother Bob in 1941, Bill had exchanged a promising Colonial Service career in the Gold Coast – Ghana – for sheep farming. Monica, who belonged to the British community in Montevideo, was returning from a visit to Gloucestershire, where her forebears had farmed for many generations. She and John were married in 1955.

Life in the Falklands presented an extreme contrast to the pleasant city life of Montevideo. Not much had been done in recent years at Hill Cove in the way of modernization; cooking, for example, was still done on a peat-burning stove which had a habit of going out every ten minutes or so. John's duties, too, often required him to stay away from the main farm settlement for several days on end. When this happened the two would have long telephone chats in the evenings in Spanish. This was for the sake of privacy, because it was a party line, and listening in on everyone else's conversations was a prime source of entertainment on the isolated farms. It was a while before the young couple realized that talking in a language that nobody else could understand was causing some irritation among the gregarious islanders. Mrs John, the word went round, was a native!

Alison, the first baby, however, was a 'kelper', a properly born Falkland Islander. Raising a first child without someone to turn to for support and advice is never easy, although fortunately Alison was a healthy baby and there were no major crises. Monica retained affectionate memories of the warmth and kindliness of the Islanders in that isolated part of the world.

After two years at Hill Cove, however, their lives took an unexpected turn. John was asked to take on the post of manager at Estancia Condor in Santa Cruz province, south of Rio Gallegos. This land holding, the size of Oxfordshire and shearing 110,000 merino sheep, belonged to the Waldron family whose original farm, Port Howard, had been established in the 1860s on the eastern side of West Falkland, next door to Hill Cove. Eric Davies, Condor's current manager, was due for retirement soon and John, with his Cambridge qualifications, was seen as a highly desirable successor. It was an offer he could not refuse.

Life at Condor presented a different sort of challenge. Initially John was surprised to find that in a number of respects Coronel's methods of sheep management were considerably more advanced than those of the larger farm. Eventually, however, he found himself at the cutting edge of the Patagonian sheep industry, responsible for introducing a variety of new technologies. The result of this was that as the years went on Condor was much in the public eye, and Monica was called upon to provide an increasing amount of hospitality. Some of the visits were business-related and others routine courtesy calls, for both John and Monica were aware of the importance of maintaining good relations with local officialdom. Visitors might include businessmen from Buenos Aires, Roman Catholic bishops from other provinces, the main national television channel filming the work of the farm and even the provincial Governor.

A few visits, however, did not quite conform to the usual pattern. It must have been in 1976 that they received a telephone call from a British journalist. He was writing a book on Patagonia. Could he come and interview them? But Bruce Chatwin got short shrift from the Blakes, which perhaps accounts for the terseness of his report:

I passed through three boring towns, San Julián, Santa Cruz and Río Gallegos. As you go south down the coast, the grass gets greener, the sheep-farms richer and the British more numerous. They are the sons and grandsons of the men who cleared and fenced the land in the 1890s . . . And you can find, nestling behind windbreaks: herbaceous borders, lawn-sprayers, fruit-cages, conservatories, cucumber sandwiches, bound sets of *Country Life* and, perhaps, the visiting Archdeacon.

The fact is that *In Patagonia*, published in 1977, which made Chatwin's name in Britain as a travel writer, did not enjoy such popularity in the locality he was writing about.

'I think,' remarked John Pilkington, who was still picking up the pieces some ten years later, 'what set the fur flying in Patagonia was that he played his cards so close to his chest. Imagining that few copies of this, his first book, would find their way back to the isolated communities in which it was set, he gave his creativity free rein.'

It seemed that Patagonia, to Bruce Chatwin, had to be for ever a wild and romantic place. He himself was palpably on the side of the oddball and the underdog – an attitude that did not play well with everyone in that part of the world.

Meanwhile John and Monica's family had been growing – Alison was followed by three sons in succession and then another daughter – so that the task of raising a family had to be balanced with all the other demands of life at Condor. Living 'over the shop' as they did, with so much going on in their lives, it was not surprising that by the mid-1970s they began to feel the need of a place to which they could retreat from time to time. It was not long before they found what they were looking for. This was a smaller farm called Killik Aike Norte, lying along the northern side of the Gallegos River, which belonged to Carlos Felton, from another ex-Falklands family. The Blakes came to an arrangement with the old man, who had been a widower for many years, that he would be able to stay on in the Casa Grande for as long as he wished after they had purchased the farm. Then when the time came for my brother to retire and for the Blakes to leave Condor – which, like Coronel, eventually passed into the hands of Benetton – the move to Killik Aike, well prepared in advance, would be a relatively straightforward matter. They could not have anticipated that in 1981 the farm's location made it an ideal site for the Argentine army to practise amphibious landing manoeuvres well away from the public gaze.

We were looking forward to spending time there when we had completed the next stage of our journey. Meanwhile, after we had lingered over our coffee at the British Club, Monica showed us over the rest of the premises, which included a billiard room with a superb baize-covered table, still in use. By this time we realized that we had been up since 5 a.m., and San Julián already seemed far distant, both in time and in space. Bidding Monica *au revoir*, we made tracks for our hotel, setting our sights now on our morning departure for Tierra del Fuego.

12. TIERRA DEL FUEGO

The southern part of Tierra del Fuego is as different from Patagonia as it is possible for any place to be. Geographically speaking, it is where the long backbone of the Andes, running all the way down the western side of South America, curves round and ends in the sea. Instead of the endless dun-coloured expanse of pampa there are mountains, lakes, channels and a whole archipelago of small islands, not to mention a range of flora and fauna unique to that part of the world and a climate in a league all its own. Off the island known as Cape Horn, where the Atlantic and Pacific ocean systems collide, the turbulence of the water is exacerbated by ferocious gales, whipping up the sea into mountainous waves. On land, even during the summer months, a stiff breeze coming direct from the South Pole can drive the temperature down below zero within hours – and the winters are long and dark.

It is generally agreed that, once again, it was the indigenous inhabitants who provided the name for the region. 'If a distant sail appeared,' wrote Lucas Bridges in *Uttermost Part of the Earth*, 'or anything else occurred to startle those who had remained at home, they would send out a warning to those away fishing by piling green branches or shrubs on the wigwam fire . . . The early explorers of that archipelago would see these countless columns of smoke rising at short intervals for miles along the coast.' And so the land was named Tierra del Fuego – Land of Fire.

Lucas Bridges was born in Ushuaia and grew up among these Indians. It was his father, Thomas Bridges, who had broken through the language barrier and who, on his first trip there in 1863, astonished the local tribes by greeting them in their own tongue.

Nothing is known of the parentage of this remarkable man. He was adopted into the family of a clergyman, the Reverend George Despard, who, it is said, gave him the surname Bridges after Bristol Bridge, the place where he had been found abandoned as a baby. Perhaps this explains something about his attitude towards the Indians. Did the absence of a family of his own make it easier to bond with these people of a totally different culture?

'Viewing such men, one can hardly make oneself believe they are fellow-creatures, and inhabitants of the same world.' This was Charles Darwin's verdict on the Indians when the *Beagle* arrived in Tierra del Fuego in 1832. He decided that mankind existed here 'in a lower state of improvement' than anywhere else in the world.

Sooner or later somebody – this being the 'Age of Improvement' – was going to want to improve the lot of these benighted people. A former naval officer by the name of Allen Gardiner was the first in the field. He set sail for Tierra del Fuego in September 1850 with six companions, intent on bringing the Gospel to the Indians, and the party were landed at Banner Cove on Picton Island, in the mouth of the Beagle Channel.

A year later a relief vessel came across the bodies of the seven men, who had evidently died of starvation, lying near a cave on an exposed part of the coast. The people they had come to help had proved so hostile and intractable that the missionaries had been obliged to take refuge in this desolate area. One by one each man's death was recorded in the journals scattered round the bodies. Gardiner himself was the last to die, but he had left a legacy in the shape of instructions for the future of the mission – instructions that were carried out faithfully by his successors.

George Despard was the man who took up the challenge. The Patagonian Missionary Society obtained a grant of Keppel Island, one of the Falkland group, and purchased a smart topsail schooner. A mission settlement was established, and a few Indians were persuaded to stay there and introduced to a simple European lifestyle. Young Thomas Bridges, who, aged thirteen, arrived on Keppel Island with Despard and his family in 1856, was quick to absorb the language of the Indians living in the settlement. Six years later he began to compile his dictionary of the Yahgan language, a monumental work which, by the end of his life, ran to 32,000 words. This was the language which, in Darwin's opinion, 'scarcely deserves to be called articulate'.

It was on 1 October 1871 that Thomas, now ordained and with his wife Mary and baby daughter, landed in Tierra del Fuego at the mission settlement of Ushuaia, successfully established by Whait Stirling in 1869.

Behind the shingle beach the grassland stretched away to meet a sudden steep less than a quarter of a mile from the shore. Between shore and hill were scattered wigwams, half-buried hovels made of branches roofed with turf and grass, smelling strongly . . . of smoke and decomposed whale-blubber or refuse flung close outside. Round the wigwams dark figures, some partially draped in otter-skins, others almost naked, stood or squatted, gazing curiously at the little boat as it approached the beach.

On 13 March we took off from Gallegos at 9.30; it was a beautiful day. The shadow of the plane, cast on the clouds below, was encircled by a rainbow ring, which sometimes became a double one, accompanying us all the way to Ushuaia. The approach by air to the world's southernmost city must be among the most dramatic in the world. As the jet banks steeply round, jagged mountain peaks rise up on either side, seemingly too close to the fuselage for comfort. Then it swoops down to the clear, deep, ice-cold waters of the bay, just in time touching down on the peninsula that forms the airport runway.

There to meet us at the fine new terminal building was Eleanor's friend Lilián, who had no difficulty in recognizing us on account of my resemblance to my sister. She whisked us off to her small white spick-and-span house, pointing out as we drove the number of attractive new dwellings that were springing up everywhere. It seemed that in recent years Ushuaia had become an increasingly desirable place to live, and much had happened since John Pilkington's last visit here, when he remarked: 'Ushuaia . . . is hated by residents and visitors alike. Seldom have I heard a good word said about it.' I wondered, when I read this, how much these feelings derived from the town's more recent history. When the days of the mission came to an end the place became a penal colony. This cannot have made for happy associations.

Beyond any doubt, the social experiment originally devised by Allen Gardiner was a resounding success. Said Lucas Bridges:

> In twenty years, a handful of missionaries had transformed these irresponsible savages into a law-abiding community . . . Under the careful direction of Father and his fellow-workers, there had grown amongst the Yahgans a keen sense of law and order and of property rights . . . There was no police force, nor was it needed, for the unwritten laws emanating from the Mission were respected by the mass of inhabitants of the region.

But this happy state of affairs could not last. Other types of settlers had by now started to arrive, and Thomas Bridges could see all too clearly what would happen next: 'Liquor would be introduced and, powerless to continue their simple existence, the poor Fuegians would go to the wall.'

The Indians were unexpectedly vulnerable in other ways too. Sixteen years after the foundation of the mission the community were decimated by an epidemic of measles, to which they had no immunity whatsoever. 'What a change! Hamlets deserted; gardens overgrown with weeds. . . but, worst of all, a frightened, weakened tribe in mourning.'

Now it was a question of protecting the Indians against the white man.

'If I could,' said Lilián, after giving us lunch, 'I'd be delighted for you to stay with me, but unfortunately my house isn't big enough.'

We leafed through the tourist brochures she had provided for us and chose the Hostería América. She took us there, helped us negotiate for a room and left us to settle in. Later in the afternoon she came to collect us, accompanied by a small boy of four whom she introduced as Tomás, one of her grandsons.

Together we visited the Lapataia National Park, where our son George had camped in 1982. We followed trails through woodlands of Antarctic beech with their characteristically tiny leaves, now and then picking from the trees small knobs of *pan de indio* – Indian bread, the tree fungus which the Indians used to eat. It did not taste of anything very much, and the snack produced by Lilián was much more acceptable. We crossed mountain streams, ventured into a peat bog along a wooden walkway and came upon a wide expanse of lake backed by majestic mountains. By the time we got back to the car we were considerably better informed about the natural life of Tierra del Fuego – and also about our hostess.

Lilián Burlando, whose family origins were Swiss–Italian, was a psychologist currently attached to the Ushuaia law court. The increase in population during the 1980s, she explained, had brought about a necessary expansion in public services. Teachers, doctors and lawyers were all encouraged to move here – and Ushuaia, once the ultimate back of beyond, suddenly became a trendy place to be. Two daughters and a son were already established in the town when she came to join them. While still in Buenos Aires she had helped to found a group for dialogue and reconciliation between Roman Catholics and Jews, and here in Ushuaia she was running a liberal religious group founded on similar principles of tolerance and acceptance. We discovered much common ground.

Arriving back at the Hostería, we were greeted with long slow tail-wags by the large amiable St Bernard who seemed permanently on duty in the foyer. While waiting to collect our key my eye was caught by a printed paper pinned up on the wall.

ORACIÓN POSTUMA
Homenaje a los víctimas del Crucero Gral. Belgrano

It was from the naval base at Ushuaia that the *General Belgrano* had set out at the beginning of May 1982. Three hundred and sixty-eight men perished when the cruiser was torpedoed by the British submarine *Conqueror*. Written by Pablo Rodriguez for the second anniversary of the disaster, the prayer was in the form of a poem, requesting peace for the souls of the departed:

> innocent victims
> of a most unjust war
> that has caused so many deaths.

Who, I thought, could fail to say 'Amen' to that?

Wherever you go in Ushuaia, we discovered the next day, you lift up your eyes and there are the encircling mountains. We learnt, when Lilián came to collect us, that the town was just entering yet another incarnation: this time it was being reinvented as a ski resort. We climbed the mountain path behind the town until we could see the Glacier Martial, and had the chair lift been working we might have thought ourselves in Switzerland. Then we visited two luxury hotels built to international standards to cater for those who liked to ski all the year round and could afford to travel to the Antipodes to do so. We could not have found a greater contrast with the Ushuaia of Lucas Bridges's boyhood.

In the afternoon Lilián introduced us to three members of her group, and in a mixture of English and Spanish we managed to have quite a lively discussion. Then we spent the evening with young Tomás's parents, the Fotheringhams. The name had suggested to me a thin, gingery, bespectacled sort of individual, but Alex Fotheringham turned out to be a jovial, generously built Argentine without a word of English. Carina, Lilián's daughter, who conversed with us as fluently as her mother, was a lawyer, while Alex, an ex-army officer, was Director of Social Services for the whole of Patagonia. They gave us a warm welcome and plied us with Swiss fondue, prepared expertly by Alex while we gradually made the acquaintance of their five children and learnt about Alex's great-grandfather Ignacio.

Ignatius Fotheringham, a professional soldier, was a Catholic, which was why he came to fight in Argentina in 1855. He served under Rosas in the Paraguayan war of 1865–70, eventually becoming a general. His auto-biography – we were shown a copy – is now an Argentine classic, comparable with Lucio Mansilla's *A Visit to the Ranquel Indians*, which we were familiar with in its new English translation by our friend and neighbour Eva Gillies. We were interested to learn that the two men were contemporaries and friends.

Ignacio's father – Alex's great-great-grandfather – had fought at Waterloo under Wellington. He was a gifted man who played the flute and had considerable skill with watercolours. The family possessed a dozen of his sketches; most of these were in Buenos Aires, but they had two in Ushuaia.

They took them off the wall to show us. We found ourselves looking at two remarkably familiar views of the Sussex coast, one of the town of Hastings and the other the small fishing village of Eastbourne. Both were dated 1816.

'These could be pretty valuable,' we said, for we knew the sort of prices that were charged for early prints in the antique shops of Lewes – and these were originals. But here, down at the bottom end of the globe and in a completely different context – how could a value ever be put on them?

We turned to other topics, such as the rights and wrongs of the Indian question. Alex, a no-nonsense ex-soldier, deplored the trendy, pro-Indian attitude that currently seemed so prevalent – but he had little support from either his wife or his mother-in-law, who quietly insisted on a more humane approach. It was strange to find ourselves still discussing our attitudes towards these tribes, now long gone, whose memory still haunted the place.

In 1886 Thomas Bridges horrified the South American Missionary Society by handing in his resignation. The decision was not lightly taken, but he had the support of a few people who were prepared to back him in his new venture. He reasoned that the first stage of mission development was at an end, and what was now required was a place which could offer steady employment for all those Indians who were willing to work, not to mention protection against the increasing depredations of the white man. With his two elder sons, Despard and Lucas, he surveyed the coastland east of Ushuaia and selected one of the many peninsulas that seemed most suitable for settlement. After a journey to Buenos Aires which included a personal interview with President Roca, he was granted eight square leagues of land for farming. He named the property Harberton, after the Devon village where his wife had been born, and in April 1887 the entire Bridges family, together with a number of Yahgan families, moved there from Ushuaia. Tommy Goodall, one of Thomas Bridges's great-grandsons, still manages the *estancia* there today.

On 15 March we headed off on an expedition to the lakes Escondido and Fagnano in a minibus with a cheerful driver by the name of Martín and with ourselves the only passengers. On the way east out of Ushuaia, as we passed three factories – Sony, Grundig, Philco – we learnt how the government had poured money into the town. The first two had employed about a thousand people each; then demand had plummeted, and now only a small workforce remained.

But soon we were up among the mountains, skirting wide expanses of soft rust-coloured bog terrain, impassable at this time of year. In winter, however, frozen and snow-covered, these wastelands were becoming a venue for winter sports. We passed a dog-breeding centre, for dog-sleighs were popular. A new ski-lift had just been completed, and there was even an illuminated ski-piste to provide more skiing time during the depth of the Fuegian winter.

One import from the northern hemisphere, however, had turned out to be just too successful. Wherever you look in this part of Tierra del Fuego, you notice that the uniform green of the mountain forests is marred by the silvery grey of dead tree-trunks, the work of the Canadian beaver. In 1947 twenty-five pairs were brought in to create a fur trade, but the absence of natural predators led to the inevitable population explosion, and now there are 50,000 of the creatures, all busily felling trees for their lodges and dams.

At last we reached Lago Escondido – the Hidden Lake. Here we were able to get out and follow a lakeside path to a hotel built on the shore further on, a peaceful stroll of about forty minutes. Then we rejoined the minibus for the last part of the outward journey, running alongside the waters of the great lake called Kami by the Indians, which is six miles across at its widest point and over forty miles long.

It was exactly 101 years before – March 1898 – that the first white men set foot in this region: the three Bridges brothers, Despard, Will and Lucas, with two Indian guides. This was the territory of the Ona, the tall, warlike guanaco hunters who were feared by the shore-dwelling canoe tribes. By this time the Bridges family at Harberton had been able to convince the Ona that their intentions – unlike those of some of the Europeans who were starting to establish themselves in the northern part of Tierra del Fuego – were entirely peaceful. There had already been skirmishes between the Indians and some of the new settlers who wanted the grazing for their sheep and were starting to clear the guanaco off the land they regarded as theirs. Any Indian who happened to get in the way was regarded as fair game.

My grandfather, writing to his mother about San Julián in October 1897, did not share this attitude:

There were five [Araucanian Indians] employed on the station when I was there . . . Many of them have become good shearers and earn the same wage as white men. They are wonderful hands among stock; their sight is so acute, for instance with a little training they learn to pick out a sheep just touched with scab more quickly than a white man . . . In Tierra del Fuego the Indians are shot down; in Patagonia they are treated as equals and are useful members of society. Last winter there were ten or twelve tents pitched on the north side of our run – that means probably 60 people; they lived quietly and did no damage, but rather good, as they killed a lot of pumas.

The waters of the great lake were like stainless steel, with occasional gleams of brightness when there was a break in the clouds overhead. We went and stood on the jetty and peered westwards where the water vanished into the distance. On the northern side the wooded mountain slopes came right down to the water. With the exception of the road, and the small settlement at the head of the lake, this part of Ona-land still seemed to be much as the Bridges brothers had first found it.

Nowadays the lake is known as Lago Fagnano, named after Monsignor Fagnano, head of the mission of Silesian Fathers who were given a grant of land on the north-western coast of Tierra del Fuego. The mission was set up for the benefit of the Indians – but the regime was of a very different kind from the one that had been developed in Ushuaia. There was no nonsense here about letting the Indians do their own thing. It was a question of bringing them under control, dressing them in European clothes – second-hand and not always a good fit – and confining them to the mission settlement. Lucas Bridges commented:

It is said that some of the settlers paid five pounds for every Indian taken off their hands and transported to a mission . . . It could be regarded as condemning free natives – rightful owners of the land – to a kind of penal servitude . . . Liberty is dear to white men; to untamed wanderers of the wild it is an absolute necessity.

Our return journey was a matter of sunshine, showers and rainbows – one of which I managed to capture on film – and, tucked away in a valley, a beaver dam.

As we stepped out the following morning a minibus came driving past with a full load of passengers; it was Martín, our guide from yesterday, who waved and hooted triumphantly. We spent an interesting morning in the Maritime Museum, where the history of the place is encapsulated in its maps and its ships. The exhibitions were housed in part of the buildings that formed the Penitentiary – but the need to make the place attractive to tourists meant that it was difficult to form an impression of the grim place that it must once have been.

In the afternoon we met Lilián at her office, and from here we all boarded a minibus for the trip to Harberton. The track branched off from the mountain route we had followed the day before and continued through many miles of woodland until it came out on the shores of the Beagle Channel and ran for some miles along the coastline. With the lovely afternoon light and the unusually calm, windless water it was an extraordinarily peaceful scene. As we rounded a corner there on the shores of the next creek lay the white, red-roofed buildings of Tierra del Fuego's first farm settlement. There was that feeling of homecoming that you get when you see at a distance the buildings, the place of your destination.

Other visitors were there, who had evidently arrived by boat. This was still a proper working farm, however, with a well-tilled vegetable patch and a good-sized shearing shed. The large, comfortable house looked out across the water, surrounded by lawns and shrubs like any English garden. Framing the gate, however, was something that took me straight back to the cathedral at Port Stanley: a white whalebone arch.

At the jetty a boat was just embarking on a wildlife tour, and Jeremy and I climbed aboard. We eased out into the waters of the Beagle Channel and soon came to a rocky islet where the black-and-white king cormorants, familiar to me from my Falklands trip, could be seen roosting on narrow cliff-shelves high above us. We passed a single albatross paddling through the water and arrived at the penguin beach. The small Magellanic penguins, endearing as ever with their downy chicks, took not the slightest notice of the motor-launch as it bobbed about a few yards offshore. Behind them could be seen the taller shapes of gentoo penguins. The colony was small compared with those in the Falklands, but it was enough to delight everyone on board.

Back on land again, we joined a group heading up the slope behind the farmstead. Threading our way along a woodland path, we arrived at a clearing where there were two small structures of woven branches. A notice explained that these were replicas of Indian wigwams. They faced on to a semicircular mound that crunched underfoot; it was one of the famous middens of bones and mussel and limpet shells, a feature of all Yahgan encampments, some of them many generations old, leaving an indelible mark on the land they had once inhabited.

'Is it possible to have a word with Thomas Goodall?' I asked one of the guides on our return to the settlement. We thought we had sighted him earlier, in gum-boots and dungarees, on the jetty, and, although not wishing to be importunate, I hoped to reaffirm the link between our two families.

A month after the three Bridges brothers had made their first trip into Ona-land, their father embarked for Buenos Aires on a journey from which he was not to return. Thomas Bridges was only fifty-five when he died. The young men, all in their twenties, resolved there and then to carry on his work: to look after their mother and sisters and do their best for the Indians, who were coming increasingly under threat. As the years went by more and more Ona arrived at Harberton with the same request: for the family to come and settle further north, for they knew that on Bridges land they would have both freedom and security. Lucas was more than ready to strike out and establish a new base in Ona-land, but by 1900 both his brothers had got engaged to be married and did not share his enthusiasm. Eventually it was agreed that he should be free to pursue the new venture, and with a team of Indians he at once set about making a trail from Harberton to the hill of Najmishk on the Atlantic coast. The distance was fifty miles as the crow flies but considerably longer on the ground, and the trail, with many interruptions and adventures, took about two years to complete.

The second Bridges family settlement, starting off with a single hut, was called Viamonte: it was this farm that our son George had visited in 1982. Hitch-hiking back from Ushuaia, he arrived at the *estancia* and asked for permission to camp on their land. By this time it was mid-April and nights were starting to get chilly, so he was taken in and given a bed for the night. He spent the evening with members of the Bridges family, in a comfortable chair in front of the central wood-burning stove.

'Who was there?' I asked him on his return to England, wondering if I might recognize a familiar name.

'I don't know who they all were, but one was called Beatle.' Six years previously, in this self-same sitting-room, of which a picture appears in his book, Bruce Chatwin had been talking with Beatle about flying saucers.

Until 1914 and the outbreak of the First World War Lucas remained in charge at Viamonte. In 1907 he was joined by his brother Despard and sister Bertha and their respective families, while their mother and Will and his family remained at Harberton. In course of time Will's daughter Clarita married John Goodall, and now their son Tommy was carrying on the family enterprise – only without the Indians.

Amazingly, there he stood in front of us, his eyes beaming behind his spectacles.

'I'm John Blake's younger sister,' I explained. 'I wrote you a rather garbled letter; I don't know if you ever got it, but anyway I just wanted to say hello, and to meet you both.'

Tommy said that Natalie, his wife, was in Ushuaia at the moment. Although reputedly a shy man, he seemed to be quite at home with us. After we had returned from a guided tour round the garden and part of the house he reappeared and said that he had rung Natalie and told her to expect us.

On the journey back everybody on the minibus seemed to share the same feeling of contentment. The calm, sunny day concluded with a truly magnificent sunset which we had to stop and photograph, and we did not get back to Ushuaia until after nine o'clock. Lilián, who already knew Natalie, took us straight round to the Bridges' town house.

The first thing we saw as we stepped inside the door was an entire marine skeleton – dolphin or small whale – slung from the ceiling, a decorative if unusual piece of interior décor. For Natalie Prosser, to give her maiden name, was an American marine biologist of some distinction. A calm, strongly built person, she received us courteously in spite of the late hour – and in spite of the fact that she had to leave at 6 a.m. the following morning to go and identify a whale that had got stranded off the coast at Río Grande. She made us welcome with a cup of tea and no sign that our visit might have been in any way intrusive.

On our last day in Ushuaia we sampled the World's End Museum, the Museo del Fin del Mundo. Here, among magnificent wildlife displays and pictures of long-vanished Indians, there was a photograph of Thomas Bridges, 'that sick, indomitable man', as his son described him. Throughout his later life he suffered from bouts of illness, brought on, one is inclined to suspect, from exhaustion and the sheer magnitude of the task he had undertaken. It was a thin, intense face, with broad forehead and eyes set wide apart. When he arrived here in 1871 there were seven to nine thousand indigenous inhabitants: Yaghans, Alacaluf, Ona and Aush. Awkward, quarrelsome, even murderous they might have been, but they were also warmhearted, courageous and extraordinarily skilful. By 1947, his son Lucas estimated that there were 'less than a hundred and fifty pure-blooded Indians and possibly a slightly larger number of half-breeds'. And in 1976 Bruce Chatwin went to Puerto Williams, the Chilean naval base on Navarino Island, to meet Grandpa Felipe, the last of the pure-blooded Yaghans, who had been born in the mission at Ushuaia.

The weather was starting to revert to normal for the time of year: a chill wind homed in on the chinks in our windproof gear. We spent the afternoon with Lilián, taking a last stroll along green footpaths on the western side of

Ushuaia before driving to the airport. As we began to turn off the main road, another car came hurtling towards us out of Ushuaia.

'It's Carina!' exclaimed Lilián. Her daughter jumped out as we reached the airport building and ran towards us waving a large brown manila envelope. It contained photocopies of the two Fotheringham watercolours of Hastings and Eastbourne.

13. KILLIK AIKE

The plane's arrival at Ushuaia was delayed, with a consequent effect on our departure.

'We'll be fine,' we said to Lilián, but she insisted on staying with us until it was time to board. There was still much to talk about, and it was evident that she valued the encouragement she had received from us in what must often have been an isolated situation. In setting up her discussion and meditation group she was, after all, breaking new ground in Tierra del Fuego, and we were glad to offer such support as we could.

It was after dark by the time we reached Gallegos; it felt like another country. However, the familiar forms of John and Monica were there to greet us, and we clambered aboard their four-wheel-drive pick-up for the hour's run to Killik Aike Norte. *Aike* is a Tehuelche word meaning watering hole or spring. A number of these Indian place-names are scattered around the southern part of Patagonia, and I used to enjoy stringing the names together: Lai Aike, Mulak Aike, Chimen Aike, Ouren Aike, Moy Aike, Guer Aike. . . I would have been delighted with this new addition to my collection, which tripped so neatly off the tongue.

The Casa Grande was a handsome two-storey building with large rooms and fine parquet floors. Our bedroom was on the ground floor, complete with its own elegant Edwardian bathroom. Elsewhere in the house I was able to discover items of furniture familiar to me from my childhood, such as my mother's desk and her Broadwood piano.

The following day was fine and sunny, and it was pleasant to breakfast in the new *quincho*, a conservatory-style room with cooking facilities at one end for alfresco meals. Then we stepped out into the bright morning, through a shady avenue of trees beyond which lay the shearing shed. Parked alongside it were two enormous trailer lorries with a small remote-controlled crane that was lifting and manoeuvring the ton-weight wool bales into place. These were wrapped not in the brown hessian sacking of my childhood but in pale gleaming polythene, the usual covering material of these days, introduced first at Condor. As John showed us round the small, compact shearing shed he explained to us the intricacies of the global wool market. Where once these bales might have ended up in Britain, this year's clip was going to a specialist firm in Finland.

Later in the day we were able to explore the extensive gardens, abundant at this time of year with flowers, fruit and vegetables and kept well irrigated with water pumped up by the constantly turning windmills. As John remarked, 'Anything will grow here as long as it gets enough water' – and this latest venture into growing organic vegetables was proving extremely successful, as evidenced by a ten-pound cauliflower. We were surprised, in this cooler climate, to see an apricot tree with its bright orange fruit just ripe on the branch and a fine patch of globe artichokes. This end of the garden looked out over the Gallegos River, and through the gate an inviting path led down to the beach. The tide was out; we could see the place where a net could be set to catch fish coming up on the rising tide and clambered over the rocks in search of the famous dinosaur fossils that had aroused so much interest in archaeological circles.

'I thought we'd have tea outside,' said Monica, bringing out a well-loaded tray. We sat round in the time-honoured English way – except that Monica and John were drinking bitter green *maté* instead of tea. Our conversation explored the activities of the British Community Council and the work of its social fund, which included supporting the British School in Gallegos and provision for ageing British pensioners. John had been district chairman for twelve years, and it was for this that he had received his OBE. As he talked about these matters I was struck by his resemblance to our father.

There were many opportunities during the next few days for catching up on what had been happening over the years, and in between we were able to explore the farm settlement. One afternoon we went over the low hill facing the Casa Grande, christened the Golden Hill on account of its aspect in the evening sun. There in the next valley lay another garden, completely deserted. Apparently Carlos Felton had had this one made as a sort of charitable venture, with its produce to be given to the poor. Masses of pears hung from unpruned branches. We lay down in the sunshine on the fallow, sheltered ground while a bird serenaded us with a bewildering variety of song-styles. 'That would be a *calandria*,' said John when we told him about it later.

One evening we watched film footage that was very familiar to me, although Jeremy was seeing it for the first time: scenes from Coronel during the 1930s, including gathering, shearing, dipping and a few shots of ourselves when small. An unforgettable shot showed the old *chata*, loaded with bales, being pulled by a team of a dozen horses. John had had the elderly film remastered for video so that the old images had been given a new lease of life. Another evening was devoted to scenes of life at Condor – and once we talked about the Falklands war.

John and Monica were driving down from Comodoro to Río Gallegos when news of the invasion came over the radio. They stared at each other in horror. The nightmare scenario – which those who could read the signs had been warning the British government about for months – was starting to unfold.

John decided to fly to Buenos Aires to confer with other senior members of Argentina's British community so as to determine what their collective reaction should be. The British Community Council had been receiving requests from the Argentine government to send delegations both to Britain and to the Islands to put the Argentine point of view. A small group of Britons from Buenos Aires had already been persuaded to visit the Islands and got, according to John Smith in Stanley, 'a very cool reception from the locals'. Another observer, 'Nap' Bound, described the meeting thus: 'People were so angry that at one stage it almost broke into open violence and all you could hear were cries of "Get out, and stay out!"' In Argentina, the British Community Council decided not to send anyone anywhere, and issued a carefully worded statement to that effect.

Back in Río Gallegos, meanwhile, tension was mounting. The roads were crammed with troops, and people in general were quite panic-stricken. The Task Force was now on its way, and since the anti-British propaganda of the time was highly imaginative in its accusations it did not occur to anyone that an act of attacking the mainland was very different from an attack on the Islands.

At Condor things were relatively quiet apart from a company of soldiers deployed in different parts of the farm. A battalion of 1,300 soldiers, however, had been billeted on Killik Aike, with the colonel and majors in the Big House. With John's presence needed at Condor, Monica was often required to stay over at Killik Aike to keep an eye on the situation.

'How on earth did you manage?' we asked in amazement.

Monica smiled her sweetest smile. 'I was extremely polite,' she said. These tactics worked like a charm: by the end of their stay all the officers were docilely removing their footwear at the front door of the Casa Grande so as not to mark the parquet floors.

Life tended to revolve round the radio. They would listen during the day to the two Argentine radio channels, tuning in from time to time to Radio Nacional Chile or news bulletins from Uruguay for alternative versions. In the evenings, however, they were able to receive full BBC coverage of events – and after that did their best to reconcile the various accounts which often differed widely. Even loyal, patriotic citizens were sometimes taken aback by these discrepancies. One night the official news bulletin reported that after the day's air sorties there had been no Argentine casualties. Yet a listening group of pilots in San Julián were only too well aware that three of their number had not returned.

The Argentine media, however, were careful not to encourage anti-British sentiments. Accusations were directed against the Thatcher government rather than the British people as such, and not at all against local residents and descendants. The result was that people in general felt sympathetic towards them as being in a difficult position, and there was no personal animosity. On the contrary, the behaviour of the military in general, who had already not endeared themselves to the public at large, and local troops in particular, who seemed to think they were already at the front and were acting accordingly, prompted many Argentines to be entirely pro-British in their sympathies.

When, however, Pope John Paul II confirmed his six-day visit to Britain at the end of May 1982 – the first Pope in office ever to visit the British Isles – there was consternation among devout Catholics. They had been led to believe by their own hierarchy that it was not a mortal sin to kill in 'defence of the Malvinas'. So why was His Holiness now going out of his way to bless the belligerent British? Argentina's claim to the Falklands, based ultimately on Papal authority, gave an extra religious edge to the Argentine war effort that might not have been apparent to the more prosaic British.

So the weeks wore on. The upbeat tone of letters written to the sons and daughter overseas – Michael in the United States and Stephen and Alison in England – did not really conceal the tensions under which John and Monica were living at this time. Meanwhile the son and daughter remaining in Argentina – Stuart, completing his military service in Gallegos, and Frances, still at school in Buenos Aires – had their own range of experiences to deal with. When the war was finally over there was plenty of mess to clear up, especially at Killik Aike – but, as with everyone else who was involved directly or indirectly in the conflict, the emotional effects were harder to gauge and took longer to disperse.

'Come and see the museum,' said John one morning. He led us to a small building not far from the Casa Grande. It was, as Anne Whitehead, who visited Killik Aike in 1994, described it, 'a neat two-storey gingerbread house, with walls clad in painted corrugated iron, two bay windows and a red roof shaded by a giant pine tree'. Inside was a remarkable assemblage of many different artefacts, each with its own story and associations. But the house itself, so we heard, had its own modest place in the records of history.

Anne Whitehead was researching the life of Mary Gilmore and wanted to have a look at the house where she had stayed for a few months in 1901. We might all be pardoned for never having heard of her, but it seemed that Mary Gilmore was a big name in Australia, where she became known as the country's poet laureate and was eventually awarded the DBE. But how did she come to be staying at Killik Aike? Anne Whitehead provided the answers. Her book, *Paradise Mislaid: In Search of the Australian Tribe of Paraguay*, came out in 1997, tracing this remarkable woman's life and her turn-of-the-century travels.

Books and bibliography came into our conversation more than once during our visit, for John was engaged in writing a book about his life and experiences in Patagonia. While he and Jeremy were in session one morning I strolled into the sitting-room and came face to face with my mother's Broadwood piano. The house was quiet, the piano was mute. I sat down and started to play. John had had it tuned recently and the tone was strong and mellow.

The piano had arrived in Patagonia with my mother in 1924 and was special because it had a metal frame. It was not the first piano to be brought out to Coronel, but the earlier one, belonging to Aunt Edith, had a wooden frame that had warped in the extremely dry climate, causing it to go out of tune. We grew up with this piano, which my mother taught us all to play. At Christmas we gathered round it to sing carols and at other times to sing traditional folk songs or Gilbert and Sullivan, for my parents had been given a complete set of the D'Oyly Carte operas, scored for piano, as a wedding present. The accompaniments were occasionally beyond my mother's capacity, but she always managed somehow.

My father could still play two short piano pieces he had learnt as a boy, but his real instrument was the harmonica, which came into its own on long car trips. He would start off at the wheel, but about half-way through the journey he changed over with my mother. Then out came the harmonica and the music: traditional English, American, Scottish and Irish tunes or perhaps a Strauss waltz. Many years later, towards the end of his life, he confessed to me that sometimes, when he was travelling alone from one part of the farm to another and had something on his mind, he used to take out the harmonica and play, steering with just one hand. If there did happen to be any other traffic, it would after all be visible from miles away.

Eleanor was the one who always remained faithful to the piano, making sure later that the gift was passed on to her daughter Penny. But when John left school and arrived in the Falklands in the late 1940s he discovered a new instrument: the piano accordion. It formed the basis of all social life in the Islands in those days and, in a word, he got bitten. The first thing he did on returning to England in 1947 was to buy an accordion, while Hugh acquired a second-hand guitar. With Eleanor at the piano and myself, aged twelve, on the drums, we were all set to provide dance music for our first Christmas party.

For the next few years the family band was a central holiday activity. We got booked to play at local village hops or wider family gatherings. When John went up to Cambridge he joined a group playing for Scottish dancing; some of these tunes were incorporated into our repertoire and simple parts were worked out for my beginner's violin. But the music of Latin America was what we enjoyed playing most.

John's departure to start his career in sheep farming meant the end of the band but not of our music. His accordion went with him and its sound was heard in many places: in the Falklands, in Patagonia and even – at a family wedding – in New Zealand. Hugh, in Bristol, organized his own Latin American band at the School of Architecture. Then he got involved in the English folk music revival, and Ruth, one of the dancers in the Bristol University folk dance team, eventually became his wife. Music-making with instruments of various kinds – guitar, melodeon, recorder, clarinet, harpsichord, Paraguayan harp – was to inform the rest of his life. As for me, I went up to Cambridge to read French and Spanish with violin and guitar strapped together, prepared for any musical opportunity that might come my way. At different times over the years singing, song-making and folk fiddling were essential forms of self-expression. And now here I was, sitting at the source of it all. I found myself playing Yradier's *La Paloma*:

> *Si a tu ventana llega una paloma,*
> *trátala con cariño, que es mi persona,*
> *cuéntale tus amores, bien de mi vida,*
> *córonala de flores, que es cosa mía . . .*

> (If to your window there comes a dove,
> I am that bird, so treat her with love,
> Tell her your heart's desire, love of my life,
> Crown her with flowers, she's something of mine . . .)

That afternoon we all went for a drive over the camp; John wanted to check out the condition of the stock. 'Coming along nicely,' he said, as a bunch of the chubby creatures scampered away from us.

A little further on I thought I could see an unfamiliar silhouette among the flock. 'Is that a . . . ?' I ventured.

'Guanaco? Yes! They're a protected species now, of course.' Time was when a bounty was paid for a pair of guanaco ears – farmers did not want them competing with their sheep for the sparse vegetation – until it was realized, just in time, that they were in danger of becoming extinct.

'Ostriches, too!' Three of the greyish-brown birds could be seen mingling with another group of sheep.

We stopped to check out a windmill. Something unexpected was propped up inside the empty circular water tank.

'That's not a solar panel, surely?'

'Certainly is! It's worth trying these things out, and not just relying on wind all the time.'

This willingness to work with new technologies was one of the qualities that in 1990 had won John the prestigious Massey-Ferguson Prize, awarded annually for significant contributions to Argentine agriculture. He had while at Condor been one of the first sheep farmers in Santa Cruz province to introduce the practice of artificial insemination, which had enabled him to develop the new breed known as the Cormo Argentino, a dual-purpose animal bred for meat as well as for wool. He was currently moving towards totally organic production, although, as he explained, this process was more complex than one might expect.

As we arrived back at the settlement a shepherd came riding in from the camp, a common enough sight in those parts with his black beret, baggy *bombachas* and sheepskin-covered saddle. It was a style of dress that did not seem to have changed in fifty years. Why should it? I found the sight overwhelmingly reassuring.

It was still dark when a car arrived for us at 7 a.m. the next day. There was one sightseeing trip that we had been advised not to miss if we were ever in that part of the world: a visit to the Perito Moreno National Park. The remoteness of this area meant that it was only during the last thirty years that it had been developed as a tourist attraction – certainly we at San Julián in the 1940s knew little if anything about it. Now, however, it had been designated a UNESCO World Heritage Site.

The car's driver, Joaquín Fernández by name, had a long association with the Blake family, dating from the time when, as they were making an emergency trip into Gallegos to take three-year-old Alison to the doctor, their vehicle skidded in the snow and overturned. Joaquín, driving past in an oil tanker, had come to their rescue.

'And you've kept in touch with him ever since!' I exclaimed.

'Well, *he* kept in touch with *us*,' said John. At any rate, Joaquín was always glad to do any driving for the family. He was a lively conversationalist, full of questions about life in Britain, not all of which I was able to answer. Meanwhile, as we headed north-west, the sun came up in a superb blaze of colour. Not long after that we caught sight of a whole herd of guanaco grazing on the open pampa, and I was able to get a couple of pictures before they fled away into the distance.

At Esperanza we stopped for a coffee and roll before continuing our journey through endless, monotonous, bush-speckled terrain. Variations in scenery were infinitesimal until, after an hour or so, we came over the brow of a hill and halted at a lay-by. Climbing out to stretch our legs, we saw a vast panorama spread out ahead of us with a line of blue far away on the horizon and, behind it, something that could have been clouds, or mountains, or both. It was our first sight of Argentina's great southern lake district, with the Andes in the distance beyond.

About midday we had another break in the town of Calafate, on the shores of Lago Argentino. Our road continued alongside the lake, branching at length on to a peninsula, where we found ourselves skirting another intensely blue sheet of water. From time to time we caught sight of large white objects – How large? It was hard to say – floating in the water. Then we rounded a corner and there it was in front of us: the vast crumpled bluish-white expanse of the Perito Moreno glacier, sixty metres high and forty kilometres across, stretching back and back into the foothills of the Andes.

'There must be a quarry somewhere near by,' was the thought in my mind as we got out of the car, for there seemed to be extensive blasting going on. Every five minutes or so there was a rumble and a roar: frequent charges of dynamite shifting many tons of rock. It was not until we had got on to the wooden viewing platform and confronted the great wall of ice that we understood what was going on. Before our eyes a vast chunk of ice began to crack and split away from the main mass, crashing into the blue-green water far below. Ice debris conglomerated at the foot of the glacier as, at intervals along the frozen ramparts, other masses exploded in a puff of rime and thundered into the water. We understood that the process, known as calving, was accelerated today on account of the warm weather and, caught up in a sort of catch-as-catch-can, we spent some time and film trying to capture the exact moment when the great chunks started to break away.

Looking down on the aquamarine water, I watched a minute moving object heading for the ice-wall, coming close but not too close. This was the alternative route to the site – by boat. But how tiny the vessel was! It was only then that we were able to take in the truly gigantic proportions of the glacier. It was not the biggest, either: the Uppsala glacier further north was even more extensive.

There was a good deal of coming and going on the three-tiered viewing platform, which had been built for safety a number of years previously after a total of some twenty people, mesmerized by the spectacle, had got too close and been killed by falling ice. The people here today were of many different ages and nationalities, but we all shared that same feeling of awe and amazement – for a moment, perhaps, reduced to our proper place in the scheme of things.

The Argentine government made full use of their national treasure during the millennium celebrations of the following year, when the glacier featured in the televised round-the-world link-up with, for added effect, an orchestra playing on a platform on top of the glacier. I could not help wondering then how they had managed it, for I knew that low temperatures can do strange things to the tuning of musical instruments.

Our drive back was memorable, too, with the brilliant blue of the great Lago Argentino set against the scorched yellow slopes and arid, dun-coloured folds of the surrounding hills. The sunset was equally spectacular, and we reached Killik Aike as we had left it, in the dark. The farm gate was shut, so we clambered over it, to the amusement of our new friend Joaquín, and rushed into the house in a great wave of enthusiasm – perhaps not entirely suitable to people of our age and station in life.

The next day was suddenly much colder. We were conscious that here there was no warming Gulf Stream to cushion this region against the onset of winter – and also that our visit was drawing to a close.

'You're lucky to be here at this time,' said John. 'There's a special tide today.' He went on to explain that twice a year the Gallegos River experienced the same phenomenon as the Severn Bore: a rapidly rising tidal wave funnelling in at extraordinary speed – the third highest tidefall in the world. At mid-morning the four of us were standing on the slope beyond the garden overlooking the beach. We concentrated on the expanse of sand and thin line of water in front of us. Birds came and went, their plumage showing white against the low cliffs in the near distance.

'There!' shouted John. 'Can you see it?' We screwed up our eyes and thought we could. A minute later, there it came: a thin ripple travelling up along the sand at incredible speed. Within a remarkably short space of time the low sandbanks had disappeared and the whole area was covered in water.

The chill wind blew harder and it came on to rain. Just the day before, at Perito Moreno, we had been picnicking out of doors on a sunlit, grassy slope.

We said our goodbyes to Killik Aike at two o'clock the following day. The plane was not leaving until that evening, but we had a rendezvous in Gallegos first.

'I think I'll leave you ladies to get on with it,' said John as we arrived at Keokén. However, he remained to help Monica in the small kitchen at the back of the craft shop while Jeremy and I went to stock up on supplies to take back with us to Buenos Aires.

Not long after our return the first two guests arrived, and we were enveloped in big hugs. After fifty years I could still recognize Pat Aldridge and Anne Bain, old schoolmates from St Hilda's. Naomi O'Byrne came in soon after, with Roberta Steele, whom I last remembered as a bright-eyed five-year-old; her parents, Ronald and Daisy Lambert, had been on the neighbouring farm of Darwin at San Julián. While Monica saw unobtrusively to everyone's needs, the conversation ran on non-stop. There was so much to catch up on after fifty years, as well as the shared experiences of our early days – memories of the old Phoenix Hotel where so many of us used to stay and of those marathon airline journeys up and down the coast.

'It was always so unfair,' said John. 'When Hugh and I got on at San Julián, you Gallegos girls were always in the proper seats, and we had to sit in those folding seats in the aisle!'

'It wasn't unfair,' said Anne, 'because we had further to go. Anyway, you could always stretch your legs when we got out to eat.'

'Oh,' sighed Naomi, 'those dreadful cold boiled chicken-legs!'

I was interested to hear from Roberta that she also was teaching English – in her case, to young children. It was obvious why so many people were involved in this activity. Whereas in the early days English was as commonly spoken as Spanish in this part of the world, nowadays it was not enough to assume that children would pick up the language naturally within the family; a conscious effort was having to be made to ensure its continuance. I recalled that even we, with our all-British upbringing, had been starting to speak 'Spanglish' before we left for England. By now the process had become accelerated, so that in many families of British descent Spanish was now predominant. Hence the establishment of the British School in Gallegos, where Lidia's son Derick was teaching. It was all the more important because some of the British families no longer had direct links with the United Kingdom. The vagaries of the wool market meant that not everybody could afford the travel fares and were therefore virtually marooned here.

Over in the Falklands, to be sure, there were native English-speakers in plenty – but they might just as well have been located in the northern hemisphere for all the communication that existed between the two communities.

The tea was all drunk, the cakes were all eaten, and although we still had not had our fill of talk Gallegos airport began to loom in our minds. I asked Naomi to take my love to the two sisters-in-law, Dorothy Mann and Mary Pickering. The party ended on a happy note, which lasted throughout the drive to the airport, and John and Monica waited to the last to see us on to the plane.

At 11.30 p.m. we were coming down over Buenos Aires with its jewelled necklaces of lights, and stepping out into its warm humidity. By midnight we were at the flat. As we opened our suitcases and burrowed into them we were astonished to feel how cold our clothes were, as if they still retained the temperature of the climate we had just left.

14. CENTENARY

Two days later we were turning the key in the lock of our own front door. The journey in space and time had been accomplished, and now we were glad to be home.

I remember once, years ago, defining 'home' to myself as 'the place where you spend your childhood'. Coronel, of course, was the place I had in mind. A few years later, however, I realized that it was not quite as simple as that. 'Home is where your parents are' served me well for a time, until I was ready to leave that home and start one of my own. 'Home', after that, became a succession of places – for we have moved six times during our married life and still do not know whether we have yet reached what the Chinese call our 'death house'. Yet the blueprint of the original home, the original Eden, had continued to remain intact in my mind.

As we began the business of unpacking we discovered that we had brought back with us a vast amount of material. It was not just a question of photographs and material souvenirs but a treasury of memories, connections, associations: a whole part of my life that I had been cut off from and which had now been restored to me. But it was going to take a while to assimilate all that I had experienced – the impressions of so many different places, the encounters with so many people, the readjustments to be made after so many years.

The physical changes that had taken place on the farm – I found that I could cope with these, after the initial shock. The important thing was, it was all still *there*, and I had been and seen it for myself. But I knew that the experience would have been much more difficult to deal with without the help of our sympathetic guide and interpreter Lidia. I had felt at the time that she was attuned to the range of feelings that I was experiencing, and I thought I understood why.

When, at the age of eleven, I stood overlooking the settlement and felt the pang of parting, it had seemed to me, with the inevitably self-centred perspective of the child, that these feelings were entirely personal to myself. Since then, however, I had come to realize that I was just one of a considerable company of people who had all been through the same experience – who had also, as it were, been cast out of Eden. I called to mind all those who had been born, lived or worked at Coronel, whose lives were rooted in the place and who had been obliged to sever all contact with it when the farm was sold. A necessary commercial decision had had profound human repercussions.

I never heard any complaints. The nearest we ever got to hearing any expression of feeling was the information that, while some of the former residents had at various times revisited the farm, others still could not bring themselves to do so. Maybe, if we had asked, we might have heard more – but our time at San Julián was after all limited, and I should have wanted to be a little surer of the ground before embarking on such a sensitive topic.

Nothing, however, had been able to keep us from that most therapeutic of activities: sharing our memories, re-creating the place in our minds and celebrating the life that we had in common. And while I valued enormously the opportunity to set foot physically in the garden of my childhood, what was even more valuable was the opportunity to tap into that reservoir of common memory, the inheritance belonging to everyone who had ever lived on the farm. In the end it was above all the people, with their welcome and their warmth, who had bridged the gulf of separation.

Families leaving farms: this has been a common enough experience throughout history. John and his family might have shared some of the same feelings when the time came for them to leave Condor – and a similar scenario was re-enacted within recent years just across the water.

Ever since my 1992 visit to the Falklands, Sally Blake and I had corresponded with each other. Her Christmas card of 1998 contained this information: 'We are to leave Hill Cove this coming winter. Tim has been wanting to retire for the last three or four years but I have been digging in my toes. However, the decision is now made and The Peaks is sold bar crossing T's and dotting I's. So sad. The last Blake connection with Hill Cove severed after over a hundred years.'

Sally had lived in camp all her life, and was not looking forward to moving permanently into Stanley, although 'my cousin who lives at Chartres has offered my sister and I (and husbands) a bolt-hole-cum-holiday-house – one of the unused ones in the settlement. . . My cousin had long ago offered to have my horses. I took them down a fortnight ago, and left my saddle there, too. I went to see them last weekend, and fed them and talked to them!'

Preparing for the move was no small task. 'There is so much junk, from generations of Blakes – and others!' However, a visit from Jane Cameron, Stanley's archivist, had helped to establish which documents and records were of value, and Sally was looking forward to becoming involved with the archives once they were settled in Stanley.

'I have to say', she told me in a letter of November 1999, 'that leaving Hill Cove was just one huge nightmare, but it is all behind me now . . .'

Two years later, however, she was still not mincing her words. 'I suppose one can get used to anything really, but I cannot say I like living in Stanley. I just spent too many years out in camp really. Too old a dog to change my ways or something!!!' I was reminded of Lidia, who had said that it had taken her a good two years to get used to living in San Julián.

I had hoped that we could have celebrated the tenth anniversary of my Falklands visit in the summer of 2002, when Tim was due to have a hip operation in Britain. But Sally had a bad fall and broke her left leg and ankle, so Tim had to come on his own. Our mutual cousin Mary Trehearne was able to visit him in hospital and passed on to us some interesting news: he had just been appointed the first Speaker of the Falkland Islands Legislative Council. Previously the Governor had presided over Council meetings, but its members felt that it was now time to follow the example of other Overseas Territories and appoint a Speaker from among themselves. With the encouragement of the then Governor, Donald Lamont, Tim was approached to see if he would be willing to take it on.

'Tim is thoroughly enjoying being Speaker,' reported Sally later that year, 'although at times he gets a bit frustrated that he cannot (must not) start giving his opinions on the matter in hand!'

However, although we could not meet them physically in 2002 we were able to see their faces when they appeared on television in a *Songs of Praise* programme for Remembrance Day featuring the Falklands. In it they recalled their unexpected visitor Hector Luna, the Argentine pilot who had been shot down over Hill Cove and whom they looked after in their own house. It would never have occurred to either of them to do anything else, enemy or not.

Meanwhile, in the year 2001 San Julián celebrated its centenary. Planning for the event had started as early as April 1997 when a small committee met and decided to produce a book to mark the occasion. When John made enquiries about arrangements he was invited to contribute some family history. It later transpired that the launching of the book would mark the beginning of the celebrations on 15 September and that the first twenty-six settler families were to be presented with a copy.

John and Monica drove up from Gallegos that day and spent some time rediscovering old landmarks in the town. This was unfamiliar territory to Monica, and John had not been there for many years. He described the visit in a family letter.

And so to the Talía, still used as a cinema with a quite respectable stage . . . The book was duly presented, with speeches, and then the older families were called up in groups of four; I was in the second group, after Hope, Kyle, Wallace and Reed, all of whom had settled land before Munro . . . Then afterwards it was rather like after church, everyone had by now seen more or less who was there, so much greeting and meeting while the hall slowly emptied.

This, however, was only the beginning. The next port of call was the 'Expo San Julián' down in the Plaza San Martín – the main square overlooking the sea – at the old Anónima premises that had been so long derelict.

The former show and sale room was filled with stands of all sorts, crafts and the like, mostly local, and there was a big marquee out front, with a whole lot more, mostly from all over Patagonia from Río Negro down. There has been a great increase in *artesanías* in recent years and some of them go on the road for weeks, setting up at the various towns, shows etc, and Monica met many acquaintances who come down to Río Gallegos.

Meanwhile the back premises, formerly the warehouse, now housed a large stage at one end and cabaret-style tables and a bar at the other. Performances by local ballet and folk dancers and well-known entertainers from further afield had been going on all week.

The next day, Sunday, seemed to be appropriate for some out-of-town exploration. John and Monica followed the same route that Jeremy and I had taken with Cath and Mauricio two and a half years earlier, pausing at the remains of the derelict freezer which John, like myself, had not visited since it was last working. Our respective recollections of the place were of a completely different order. He found it fascinating

to roam around and see the steam-driven main freezing compressor with a flywheel at least ten feet in diameter, the boilers and the track running down to the bay, ending in a derelict steam crane. Then we carried on, past the 'Bombas' where the freezer used to get its water from and where during the war the British community used to hold fund-raising *asados*. I can remember the Spanish residents dancing to the *gaita gallega* (the Galician bagpipes) there.

On their return to San Julián they went in search of Mary Pickering and her sisters, finally locating them at the Expo, escorted by their younger brother Duncan, who had come up from Gallegos for the occasion. Mary had fully recovered from her operation of two years ago, but Lidia was in hospital with a broken hip.

By this time, San Julián being San Julián, everybody knew who had come and several people looked us up . . . Most of the Brits of our generation spoke in English . . . It was really nice to feel that although we had always been out on the farm, the town recognized how much the multi-national community owed to *la Compañía* and the other farms around . . . San Julián does not forget that it was founded by and from the Camp, and existed for it, certainly right up till the Hudson Volcano hit in 1991.

At eleven o'clock the following morning the entire town was assembled in the main street with the band playing, awaiting the arrival of the Provincial Governor, who did not materialize until 12.30.

The worthy citizens of SJ were not pleased with the long wait while the Governor (Peronist but really a home-grown *caudillo*) flew in, in his Lear jet. The town is not very P-aligned and the applause somewhat lukewarm . . .

The Governor was none other than Néstor Kirchner, who in May 2003 was to become President of Argentina. The first President to have been born in Patagonia, of Swiss descent on his father's side and Croatian on his mother's, he was, one might say, of typically Patagonian provenance.

After the speeches came the *desfile*. This was a phenomenal march-past, involving detachments of army, navy, air force and coastguards,

followed by the schools, right down to kindergarten tots, and every cultural and sporting organization who could field a banner to march behind. There was a mock-up of Magellan's flagship *Victoria*, a float full of youngsters in folk costumes of all the countries the immigrants came from, and even the *chata* which usually sits in the main street had been properly harnessed up with a team of horses and loaded with wool bales and *pobladores* in fin-de-siècle dress. Finally the horsemen, the *gaucho* clubs and racing stables. There must have been nearly fifty – beautiful horses and gear; I was a bit anxious how they were going to like parading past the band thumping away . . . Some of them danced around a bit, but the bandmaster knew his stuff, lowered the volume of brass and percussion and all was well.

Next on the programme was the unveiling of a Centenary Monument by provincial dignitaries. John and Monica went along to this official ceremony, but the majority of the townsfolk, having had their fill of waiting, turned their backs on officialdom and their future President and headed straight for the Asado Popular, the mass sheep-roast which had been set up on the old football pitch. Mary described the scene as she, Cath and Duncan arrived:

A fine black mesh 1½ metres high was put all round the field on top of the walls as a wind break. There were tables and chairs provided for all the town by the different municipalities; also *asadores* [roasting-spits] – no town has 200 *asadores*. Two hundred lambs or hoggets were roasted. There were twenty places where the *asados* were being made, all manned by last year's graduates from the secondary school, helped by their parents. There were *mata negra* shelters round each fireplace.

Duncan had made various trips early in the morning to see how the *asados* were coming on. He said various dads were coping with them, as the main dance had been held the night before, and lots of our boys were a little groggy; thank goodness we had dads to help.

The catering arrangements evidently worked extremely well, and the meal was 'all very tasty and well cooked', although 'it was rather windy and we had to hang on to our plates'. They did not, however, stay for the dessert, 'an *alfajor* all done up into various enormous cakes' because Duncan wanted to go out to Coronel to see the shearing. Mary explained:

We are always made most welcome by Leopoldo and Ana. Duncan had never been back. He was most impressed by the way the shearing shed had been lengthened. The platform where the bales were rolled out on to, and where we all played as children, had disappeared. On one side of the building the bales were kept under cover; on the other side, all the vehicles are under cover. Sad to see no Big House. Not the same farm.

A couple of months later we took delivery of a heavy parcel almost bursting out of its envelope. This, it turned out, was the *San Julián Centenary Book*, consisting of two large volumes printed on high-quality paper and copiously illustrated. John had made a point of acquiring copies for the three of us remaining in England. It was a real labour of love.

The mastermind behind the project, we gathered, was Nohry Fueyo, a descendant of one of the early San Julián families. As a schoolteacher, she evidently kept in mind the principle of maximum involvement. Workshops and discussion groups had been set up to study the town's early history and its indigenous inhabitants, and the results were reproduced verbatim. Everything that you might ever want to know about the subsequent history of San Julián, including every institution, organization and club, in full personal and emotional detail, together with the foundation documents of the town, had all been collected together in Volume I.

Volume II was something else. It was a compendium of family histories: the stories of all those who had arrived in San Julián before 1930. No less than 209 families qualified for inclusion, complete, in most cases, with wonderful period photographs and details of descendants. Fascinated, I pored over these pages which revived so many memories of the people I had known in my childhood. What a polyglot community it was! A professional statistician would have had a field day with all this demographic material. I attempted a rough analysis of the origins of the families, including the Britons who had established the five major *estancias* that were the reason for the port's initial development. The results would not be surprising to anyone conversant with this part of Argentina but were interesting none the less.

The overwhelming majority of the town's early inhabitants were, predictably, from Spain, with many of the families forming clusters from around specific Spanish towns, suggesting that news of opportunities in Patagonia got round by word of mouth. The northern province of Asturias, a land of coal mines and steep green mountains not unlike Wales, headed the list with thirty-five families, seven of them coming from the district of Mieres in Oviedo, including the seven Fueyo brothers. Next came rainy Galicia in the north-west with twenty-one families, followed by the north-east with thirteen Basques and six Catalans. The remaining eighteen families were from different parts of Spain further south, including four from the town of Blacos in Soria.

Neck and neck in second place came the Germans (including three Austrians) and the Scots, with eighteen families apiece. No less than seven of the pioneering Scots arrived via the Falklands. These were followed closely by the Yugoslavs – the *yugos* or *austriacos* – numbering fourteen, with a cluster of five from the Croatian island of Brac.

The warmer Mediterranean countries were also represented, with eleven Italian couples, known as *tanos* – a smaller proportion than in the northern part of Argentina – six Greeks and five Lebanese, or *turcos*. Then came the ten English families – my grandfather, of course, being one of the two from the Falklands. The remaining *gringos* included one Irishman, one Canadian and one Australian – Augustus Moy, the fattest man we children had ever seen – from New South Wales. So, together with Aneurin Erasmus Jones from Trelew, married to a Basque wife (they must have had to communicate in Spanish) the contingent originating in the British Isles came to the respectable total of thirty-two.

Sixteen families came from other parts of Argentina: eight from Buenos Aires, five from Patagones, three from the sultry north. Most of these were of Hispanic origin, but there were three who were proud of their indigenous Indian roots. The nine Chileans included two from the island of Chiloé – again, original inhabitants – and the five from Uruguay rounded off the contingent of families born in South America, many of whom were second-generation immigrants anyway.

From Eastern Europe came four Russian families and one each from Poland, Czechoslovakia and the Ukraine, all indiscriminately known as *rusos*. Scandinavia was represented by one Norwegian and one Dane – both arriving via the Falklands – and the European input was completed by one representative from France and one from Switzerland.

Many of the new settlers continued to practise their original trades: builders, bakers, carpenters, mechanics, shopkeepers. A significant number, however, had a single long-term ambition: to take advantage of the boom in wool prices, buy or rent land and raise sheep. This was how the small to medium-sized *estancias* began to develop. These, however, were more vulnerable to the fluctuations of the market than the large *estancias* and in later times were badly affected by the Mount Hudson eruption.

Educating children of such diverse origins presented a considerable challenge. The local National School, started in 1908 with twenty pupils, was described by one of its most dedicated teachers – Emilio Moyano, who taught from 1915 to 1924 – as a Tower of Babel. One of his former pupils commented:

> I don't know how he got all the children to understand . . . There were the gringos with their own words, the ones we called *rusos* with theirs, the Germans, a few *tanos*, the *yugos* and the *galegos* [from Galicia] like Carmiña who always mixed up the meanings of words, provoking everyone's laughter. As for us . . . 'Well, you're no dictionaries either!' the master used to say. But we managed to communicate; that was the important thing.

In the 1920s two of the larger national groups, the Germans and the British, solved the problem by setting up their own schools, and the Germans developed a library which later evolved into an adult education institute. The British school taught in both English and Spanish. It was open to children of every nationality and was run by Miss Vernham who, my brother John recalls, 'wore long Edwardian dresses and sported pince-nez'.

She continued to live in the port after her retirement and my mother used to visit her regularly, accompanied by my sister and me if we were at home. Her white, wispy hair was done up on the top of her head in the style of a cottage loaf, and she entertained us in her small front room that also housed a harmonium and an indeterminate number of cats. The school by this time was being run by Raquel, until her move to Comodoro in 1949.

On the face of it, San Julián is probably little different from any other New World immigrant-based township. It might be said to have much in common, for example, with Garrison Keillor's imaginary North American community Lake Wobegon. But rarely, if ever, I believe, has a community of this kind been documented in such detail, full of local characters and anecdotes. It is arguable that, had the project been in British hands, it would have been a more sober affair, with strict attention to factual detail and a minimum of emotion. But where the Hispanic temperament is concerned you cannot keep feelings out of it. The result has been a warm and living evocation of a developing community – now, as John concluded in his letter, facing an uncertain future: 'All the big farms are still operating and employing labour, as is the gold mine inland at Cerro Vanguardia, and there is a certain amount of commercial fishing, but times are difficult for everybody.'

On a chilly evening in early April 2003 Jeremy and I, hastening through the streets of London, noticed across the road a number of couples heading, as we were ourselves, for the Argentine Embassy in Belgrave Square. The Anglo-Argentine Society was hosting a talk and book launch; the book, *A Story of Patagonia*, was by John Locke Blake. The event was evidently a popular one, for the Canning Room was crowded. Not only was this a big Blake family occasion but it was also of interest to Anglo-Argentine Society members from other parts of Argentina, the majority of whom would rarely if ever have ventured into the desolate regions of the south. For them, as much as for any European, Patagonia has always been *terra incognita*.

The first person we recognized on entering the building was my nephew Stuart, whose lucky raffle ticket had sent us off on our journey to Patagonia in the first place. He was in his familiar role of being in several places at once, on a variety of errands. We greeted his mother Monica, who had just finished setting up her display of woollen craft goods – then there at my elbow was John himself; but there was little time for greeting, for the seats were filling up fast. We managed to squeeze into the same row as my brother and sister, Hugh and Eleanor, and their respective spouses. The whole event felt rather like a family wedding. Just behind us, with her husband Brian, was our cousin Mary Trehearne, whose father, Uncle Robert, had been the first manager at Coronel. Mary's accurate and scholarly sifting through family correspondence led to her becoming the first chronicler of the family's sheep-farming venture, providing the definitive narrative of the early days for those of us who were carrying on the story. Next to her was another cousin I had not seen for many years: Tim's elder sister Olive, who, with her husband, had spent many years as a missionary in Papua New Guinea.

John's talk, outlining the early history of the region, was followed by a series of video vignettes of various dates, incorporating some of the old film from Coronel as well as more recent material from Condor and Killik Aike and showing typical events on a Patagonian sheep farm. The audience's reaction showed the effectiveness of this medium in conveying the fundamental aspects of the life: its vigour and vitality – sheep, horses, wildlife – as well as the sheer scale of the enterprise.

After this came the questions, which were many and varied, including an unexpected one from somebody just across the aisle: 'Can you tell us anything about St David's school in Trelew?'

An elderly lady in the row just behind the speaker sat up and showed a lot of interest. It was only after the questions were over, the vote of thanks given and we all started talking to one another that I realized this was none other than Bessie Pearce from Shropshire, now in her eighties, the only one of the Mann sisters to have settled in England. With her was her daughter Sheila, who had travelled a number of times to San Julián and helped to keep the family in touch. I was able to catch up quickly on the state of health of the San Julián sisters and then got hold of Eleanor.

'Here's Bessie!' I said. My sister flung herself into her arms for an emotional reunion. Meanwhile I began talking with Eva Hoffman, the petite dark-haired stranger who had asked the question about her old school, St David's. Her maiden name, she explained, was Bideleux, and her father, a Frenchman, had been manager of the Trelew branch of the Bank of London and South America.

'I remember the Manns from San Julián,' she went on. 'The youngest, Agnes, was a special friend of mine and often came to our house. I'd love to know what happened to her.'

'She lives in Montevideo,' I said, 'and I can send you her address.'

'We went back to Trelew in 1993, after forty-five years,' wrote Eva in a subsequent letter. 'The railway had gone, the roads were paved. The Bank's house was being demolished (now Lloyd's). I remember having a drink at the Touring Club, my father's local. I enclose a couple of computer copies of snaps taken of Agnes and friends, which might amuse you!'

The image of the rather sad-looking girl on the edge of the parting photograph taken as we left San Julián was replaced by one of a slightly older Agnes, laughing with a group of new friends – just as I had made new ones when we got to England. Life had moved on for us all, which was as it should be.

It would be impossible to detail the number of reunions that took place that evening in April, of the people who were meeting again after so many years. The threads of all our lives were gathered together at that time and in that place, as indeed they had been in the book whose launch we were celebrating. Half a century ago, a continent and a hemisphere away: friendship, as Raquel said, does not depend on time or distance.

Ten months after the book launch, in February 2004, came news of the death of Bessie Pearce at the age of eighty-three. Later that year two of her daughters, Sheila and Linda, travelled out to Argentina with her ashes. On Saturday 2 October twelve members of the Mann family drove up the familiar track to Coronel. Passing the site of the old Casa Grande, they all assembled at the top end of the garden. Sheila and Linda each took a symbolic handful of their mother's ashes and sprinkled them at the foot of the Stony Hill.

'It was the final closure,' said Sheila.

Children of Patagonia

We all grew up
in the middle of this vast landscape
and like the Indians before us
wind, dust and solitude
were the facts of our life.

In time, we children were scattered
to the four corners of the earth –
other countries, other continents –
where we settled, took root,
and raised our families.

Now, at the end of our time,
we still carry inside us
the home we once inhabited
set in that outsize wilderness
where there is space for the soul.

CHRONOLOGICAL TABLES

Chronological Table – Argentina

1492	Arrival of Columbus in the New World.
1495	Treaty of Tordesillas: Papal decree that all lands discovered west of Meridian 46 degrees 7 minutes should belong to Spain, and all those east to Portugal.
1520	Magellan celebrates mass at San Julián and spends the winter there before continuing south and finding his way through the Tierra del Fuego archipelago to the Pacific.
1578	Sir Francis Drake winters at San Julián and subsequently gets round Cape Horn and back home.
1580	Foundation of the port of Buenos Aires, serving mainly as an outlet for silver from the mines of Peru.
1776	Establishment of Spanish Viceroyalty, covering present-day Argentina, Chile, Paraguay, Uruguay and Bolivia.
1780	Antonio de Viedma establishes a colony at San Julián.
1806	Buenos Aires is captured by British forces but is retaken six weeks later.
1816	The United Provinces of the River Plate – later Argentina – declare independence from Spain.
1826	First voyage of the survey ship HMS *Beagle* down coast of Patagonia.
1837	Third voyage of HMS *Beagle*, lasting nearly five years, with Charles Darwin as resident naturalist.
1850	Allen Gardiner's doomed expedition to convert the Indians of Tierra del Fuego.
1865	Arrival of Welsh colonists in northern Patagonia.
1869	Whait Stirling establishes mission station at Ushuaia.
1871	Thomas and Mary Bridges arrive at Ushuaia.
1875	Carlos Moyano appointed Governor of Santa Cruz Province.
1876	Henry Reynard brings first consignment of sheep over from the Falklands.
1880	Moyano visits the Falklands.

1886	James Lovegrove Waldron establishes Estancia Condor on the Magellan Straits.
1893	Robert Blake spends winter at San Julián.
1899	Death of Donald Munro.
1901	Foundation of Municipality of Puerto San Julián.
1907	Robert Blake II becomes manager at Coronel.
1908	Casa Grande built; visit by Robert and Dora Blake.
1911	Arrival of Edith Blake.
1919	Arthur Blake arrives at Coronel.
1920	The Intervention.
1921	The General Strike.
1924	Arrival of Millicent Blake.
1928	Robert Blake II retires; Arthur becomes manager.
1947	Arthur retires; Blake family returns to England; Lionel Pickering becomes manager at Coronel under Arthur's supervision.
1978	Sale of Coronel to Siracusa.
1982	Falklands War and end of military regime.
1991	Eruption of Mount Hudson.
1996	Sale of Coronel to Benetton.
2001	San Julián Centenary.

Chronological Table – Falkland Islands

1592 First probable sighting of the Islands by John Davis in the *Desire*.

1690 First landing on the Islands by John Strong in the *Welfare*; the channel between the two main islands is named Falkland Sound.

1701 Second landing by French navigator Gouin de Beauchêne. The French name the Islands Les Iles Malouines.

1764 First settlement, Port Louis, on East Falkland, by Louis de Bougainville.

1765 Second settlement, Port Egmont, on Saunders Island, West Falkland, by John Byron (grandfather of the poet).

1766 The French and the British discover each other's existence.

1767 Spain claims the colony, citing the Treaty of Tordesillas. France hands it over. Les Iles Malouines become Las Islas Malvinas.

1770 The Spanish Viceroy in Buenos Aires orders the expulsion of the British from Port Egmont.

1774 Britain pulls out of Falklands, probably for reasons of economy.

1816 The United Provinces of the Río de la Plata gain independence from Spain and, as its heir, claim the Islands.

1828 Louis Vernet, with government permission, establishes a multinational colony on East Falkland.

1832 A mutiny at the penal settlement of San Carlos leads to the death of acting Governor Mestivier. The small number of British settlers appeal to their government to establish *Pax Britannica*.

1833 Captain Onslow arrives and hoists the Union Jack. The Islands are now under British rule.

1851 Establishment of Falkland Islands Company.

1854 Patagonian Missionary Society establishes a base on Keppel Island.

1856 Thomas Bridges, aged thirteen, arrives on Keppel Island.

1867 James Waldron and two other farmers take up land for sheep farming on West Falkland.

1868 Wickham Bertrand and Ernest Holmested take up land on West Falkland.

1871 Thomas and Mary Bridges depart for Tierra del Fuego.

1873 Robert Blake joins Holmested at Shallow Bay.

1880 Carlos Moyano, Governor of Santa Cruz, visits Falklands and invites sheep farmers to take up land in Patagonia.

1881 Dora Blake arrives at Shallow Bay.

1882 Hill Cove settlement built.

1892 Cathedral built in Stanley.

1898 Dora Blake and her eight children return to England.

1902	Robert II spends a year at Hill Cove before going to San Julián.
1910	Robert and Dora revisit Hill Cove.
1912	Robert and Dora revisit Hill Cove for a second time.
1952	Bill Blake succeeds Hugh Harding as manager at Hill Cove.
1953	John Blake joins Bill as assistant manager.
1958	Tim (Lionel) Blake succeeds John Blake as assistant manager.
1968	Bill Blake retires; Tim becomes manager.
1982	Falklands invaded by Argentina.
1987	Hill Cove sold to Falkland Islands Company; Tim and Sally Blake continue to farm The Peaks, part of the original farm.
1988	Tim Blake speaks at United Nations on behalf of Falklands.
1991	Falkland pastures affected by ash from Hudson volcano.
1992	Centenary of cathedral; visit by Archbishop of Canterbury; Pilgrims and Philatelists tour.
1999	Sale of The Peaks; Tim and Sally Blake retire to Stanley.
2002	Tim Blake appointed Speaker of Legislative Council.

FAMILY TREES

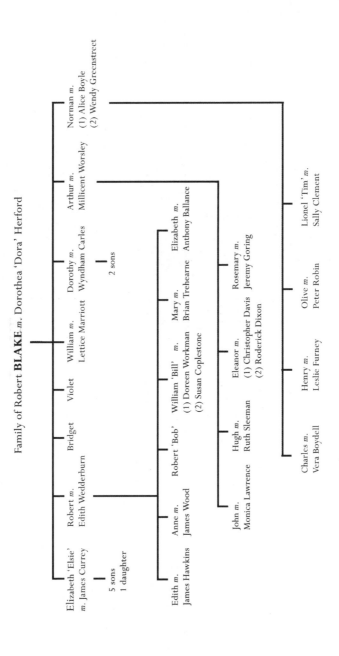

Family of Robert **BLAKE** *m.* Dorothea 'Dora' Herford

Elizabeth 'Elsie'
m. James Currey

5 sons
1 daughter

Robert *m.*
Edith Wedderburn

Bridget

Violet

William *m.*
Lettice Marriott

Dorothy *m.*
Wyndham Carles

2 sons

Arthur *m.*
Millicent Worsley

Norman *m.*
(1) Alice Boyle
(2) Wendy Greenstreet

Edith *m.*
James Hawkins

Anne *m.*
James Wood

Robert 'Bob'

William 'Bill' *m.*
(1) Doreen Workman
(2) Susan Coplestone

Mary *m.*
Brian Trehearne

Elizabeth *m.*
Anthony Ballance

John *m.*
Monica Lawrence

Hugh *m.*
Ruth Sleeman

Eleanor *m.*
(1) Christopher Davis
(2) Roderick Dixon

Rosemary *m.*
Jeremy Goring

Charles *m.*
Vera Boydell

Henry *m.*
Leslie Furney

Olive *m.*
Peter Robin

Lionel 'Tim' *m.*
Sally Clement

Family of Alexander 'Alec' **MANN** *m.* Matilda Craik

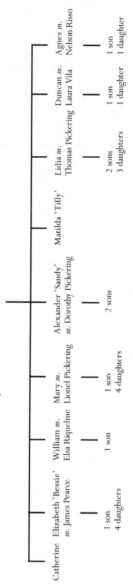

Catherine   Elizabeth 'Bessie'   William *m.*   Mary *m.*   Alexander 'Sandy'   Matilda 'Tilly'   Lidia *m.*   Duncan *m.*   Agnes *m.*
            m. James Pearce   Elsa Riquelme   Lionel Pickering   *m.* Dorothy Pickering   Thomas Pickering   Laura Vila   Nelson Risso

            1 son   1 son   1 son   2 sons   2 sons   1 son   1 son
            4 daughters   4 daughters   3 daughters 1 daughter   1 daughter

BIBLIOGRAPHY

Aloyz de Simonato, Camila Raquel, *Raigambres sureñas*
    (private printing, 1984)
Barrett, Katherine and Robert, *A Yankee in Patagonia*
    (Heffer, Cambridge, 1931)
Blake, John Locke, *A Story of Patagonia*
    (Book Guild, Lewes, Sussex, 2003)
Bound, Graham, *Falkland Islanders at War*
    (Pen and Sword Books, Barnsley, 2002)
Bridges, Lucas, *Uttermost Part of the Earth*
    (Century Hutchinson, London, 1987)
Cawkell, M.B., Maling, D.H. and Cawkell, E.M., *The Falkland Islands*
    (Macmillan, London, 1960)
Chatwin, Bruce, *In Patagonia*
    (Pan Books, London, 1979)
Darwin, Charles, *Voyage of the Beagle*
    (Penguin, Harmondsworth, 1989)
Fisher, Jo, *Out of the Shadows*
    (Latin America Bureau, London, 1993)
Fueyo, Nohry, *Centenario de Puerto San Julián, Tomos I y II*
    (private printing, 2001)
Goebel, Julius, *The Struggle for the Falkland Islands*
    (Yale University Press, Hartford, Connecticut, 1982)
Mansilla, Lucio V., *A Visit to the Ranquel Indians*, Eva Gillies (tr.)
    (University of Nebraska Press, Lincoln, Nebraska, 1997)
Mainwaring, Michael, *From the Falklands to Patagonia*
    (Allison and Busby, London, 1983)
Musters, George Chaworth, *At Home with the Patagonians*
    (Greenwood Press, New York, 1969)
Pilkington, John, *An Englishman in Patagonia*
    (Century, London, 1991)
Saint-Exupéry, Antoine de, *Southern Mail: Night Flight*, Curtis Cate (tr.)
    (Penguin, Harmondsworth, 1976)

Smith, John, *74 Days: An Islander's Diary of the Occupation*
(Century, London, 1984)
Sunday Times Insight Team, *The Falklands War*
(Sphere Books, London, 1982)
Time Out Patagonia
(Penguin, Harmondsworth, 2002)
Trehearne, Mary, *Falkland Heritage*
(Stockwell, Ilfracombe, 1978)
—, *Patagonian Harvest*
(private printing, 1989)
Whitehead, Anne, *Bluestocking in Patagonia*
(Profile Books, London, 2003)
Wigglesworth, Angela, *Falkland People*
(Peter Owen, London, 1992)

INDEX

Aa, Pieter van der, 74
Abbeville, Sarre d', 74
Aerolinéas Argentinas, 45
Aeroparque Jorge Newbery, Buenos
    Aires, 56
Aeroposta Argentina, 57
Agreiter, Monsignor Anton, 30
Albernoz, Joao Teixera, 74
Aldridge, Pat, 146
Aloyz, Julio (b. Yehuda Israel
    Yudelevich), 49, 50, 67–8, 69, 83,
    84, 85, 94, 98
Aloyz, Julito, 49, 50, 68, 69, 93, 94, 97
Aloyz, Luis, 69
Aloyz, Raquel, see Camila Raquel Aloyz
    de Simonato
Aloyz, Raquel 'Trixie', 64
Aloyz, Robertito, 64
Aloyz de Simonato, Camila Raquel,
    44–5, 49, 50, 59, 64–71, 94, 157,
    159
Amnesty International, 28
Anglo-Argentine Society, 43, 157
Anónima, San Julián, 93, 94, 152
Araucano Indians, 55, 131–2
Argensud, San Julián, 94
Argentine Embassy, London, 157
Assembly Rooms, Port Stanley, 28
Avila Star, 68–9, 106

Bain, Anne, 146
Balcón, El, Rada Tilly, 64

Baum, Señor, 95
Baum's, San Julián, 95
Bazeley, Colin, 30, 36
Beagle, HMS, 23, 74, 126, 161
Beauchêne, Gouin de, 163
Bedetou, 'Mamita', 94
Bedetou, Peter, 94
Behm, Ernest, 78, 79
Benetton, 103, 111, 122, 162
Bertrand, Wickham, 33, 163
Bideleux, Eva, see Eva Hoffman
Birmingham Settlement, 86
Blake, Alex, 29
Blake, Alison, 121, 122, 140, 143
Blake, Arthur, 14, 15–16, 24, 29, 34,
    40, 44, 58, 68, 70, 82–9, 92, 95,
    100, 104–5, 107–8, 108, 115, 116,
    118–19, 141–2, 162
Blake, Bill, 96, 120, 164
Blake, Bob, 68, 88, 89, 107, 120
Blake, Bridget, 81, 82, 87
Blake, Dora, see Dorothea Blake
Blake, Dorothea (née Herford), 65, 76,
    77, 82, 86, 112, 162, 164
Blake, Dorothy), 82
Blake, Edith (née Wedderburn), 65,
    81–8, 104, 111, 117–18, 141, 162
Blake, Elsie, 82
Blake, Frances, 140
Blake, Hugh, 7, 14, 15–16, 43, 44,
    88–9, 98, 113, 142, 146, 157
Blake, John Locke, 7, 9, 14, 15, 16,

17, 18, 29, 44, 45, 46, 47, 51, 69,
88–9, 96, 100, 101, 107, 116, 117,
119, 120–1, 122, 137–8, 138–9,
140, 141, 142, 143–4, 145, 146,
147, 150, 151, 152–4, 156, 157,
158, 164

Blake, Locke, 76

Blake, Michael, 140

Blake, Millicent (née Worsley), 14, 15,
16, 24, 34, 44, 50, 64, 65–6, 69,
86–8, 100, 104, 108, 113, 114, 118,
119, 141, 157, 162

Blake, Monica, 7, 17, 46, 116, 117,
120, 121, 122, 123, 137, 138, 139,
140, 146, 147, 152, 154, 157

Blake, Norman, 28–9

Blake, Paul, 29, 35, 36

Blake, Robert, Admiral of the Fleet, 76

Blake, Robert, 21, 29, 31, 33–4, 37,
76–9, 81–2, 86, 87, 88, 103, 110,
112, 117, 131–2, 155, 162, 164

Blake, Robert, 29, 50, 68, 81–8, 91,
112, 120, 158, 162, 164

Blake, Ruth, 142, 157

Blake, Sally, 18, 21, 22, 24, 29, 33, 35,
150–1, 164

Blake, Stephen, 140

Blake, Stuart, 7, 18, 43, 45, 140, 157

Blake, Tim, 18, 21–2, 24, 28, 29, 35,
150, 151, 158, 164

Blake, Violet, 82

Bougainville, Louis de, 163

Bound, Graham, 7

Bound, 'Nap', 139

Bridges, Beatle, 134

Bridges, David, 107

Bridges, Despard, 130, 131, 134

Bridges, Jannette, 107

Bridges, Lucas, 41, 107, 125, 127,
129, 130, 131, 132, 134, 135

Bridges, Mary, 126, 134, 161, 164

Bridges, Thomas, 41, 125, 126, 127,
130, 134, 135, 161, 163, 164

Bridges, Will, 131, 134

Bristol University, 142

British Club, Gallegos, 117, 120, 123

British Community Council, 138, 139

British Hospital, Montevideo, 118

British School, Gallegos, 138, 146

Brooks, Gwerfyl, 21, 22–3, 27, 31, 35,
42

Brunel, Isambard Kingdom, 27

Burlando, Lilián, 7, 45, 47, 127, 128,
129, 133, 135, 136, 137

Byron, John, 163

Cameron, Jane, 151

Carey, Eileen, 30, 36

Carey, Doctor George, Archbishop of
Canterbury, 22, 28, 30, 35, 36, 164

Casa Juan, Trelew, 58

Catholic Church, Port Stanley, 30

Centenario de Puerto San Julián, Tomos I y II
(Nohry Fueyo), 154–7

Chace, Ned, 81

Charles, Prince of Wales, 51, 116

Chatwin, Bruce, 9, 73, 120, 121–2,
134, 135

Child Education, 87

'Children of Patagonia' (Rosemary
Goring), 159

Christ Church Cathedral, Port Stanley,
22, 30

Clifton High School, 77

Cobb, Emily, 76

Cobb, Fred, 76

Columbus, Christopher, 161

Condor (Estancia), 16, 17, 18, 29, 33,
69, 100, 101, 119, 121, 122, 137,
139, 143, 150, 158, 162

Coronel (Estancia), 13–14, 16–17,
  33–4, 44, 50, 51, 68, 77–9, 81–5,
  86–9, 92, 93, 98, 100, 101, 103–14,
  115, 116, 117, 118, 120, 122, 138–9,
  141, 149–50, 154, 158, 159, 162
  early history of, 77–9, 81–5, 86–9,
    103–4
  breaking in horses, 110
  sheep shearing, 111–13
  buy-out by Benetton, 103, 111
  lay-out of the Casa Grande, 106–9
Conqueror, HMS, 128
Coventry, HMS, 39
Cullen (Estancia), 119

D'Arcy, Colonel George, 21, 31, 40
Dartmouth School, 77
Darwin, Charles, 23, 74–5, 79, 126,
  161
Davies, Eric, 121
Davis, John, 163
Dean Brothers, 41
Deseado Show, 87
Despard, Reverend George, 41, 125,
  126
Diana, Princess of Wales, 60
Dixon, Eleanor (née Blake), 7, 14, 15,
  43, 44, 45, 56, 88, 99, 107, 127,
  142, 157
Don Otto, Trelew, 63
Doughty, Thomas, 73
Drake, Sir Francis, 73, 161

Ein Breiniad (Our Heritage), 56
Elizabeth, Queen Mother, 81
Englishman in Patagonia, An (John
  Pilkington), 7
'Expo San Julián', 152–4
Exposición Rural, Buenos Aires, 66

Faber and Faber, 29
Fagnano, Monsignor, 132
Falkland Heritage (Mary Trehearne), 7
Falkland Islanders at War (Graham
  Bound), 7
Falkland Islands, 13, 14, 16, 18–19,
  21–31, 33–42, 75–6, 77, 79, 96,
  116, 120–1, 139–40, 142, 147, 151,
  161, 162, 163, 164
  flora and fauna, 26, 28, 37, 38, 39,
    40
Falkland Islands Association, 22
Falkland Islands Broadcasting Service,
  38
Falkland Islands Company, 76, 163,
  164
Falkland Islands Development
  Corporation, 29
Falkland Islands Government Air
  Service (FIGAS), 24, 33, 38
Falkland Islands Legislative Council,
  21, 151
Falkland Islands Newsletter, 22, 39
Falkland People (Angela Wigglesworth)
  7
Falklands War, 21–2, 25–6, 30, 36,
  37–8, 39, 47, 51, 100, 116, 117,
  139–40, 162, 164
  lead-up to, 17–19, 27–8, 122
  Argentine invasion of islands,
    18–19, 27, 139–40
  sinking of HMS *Sheffield*, 27
  sinking of *General Belgrano*, 51,
    128–9
  retaking of Goose Green, 25–6
  legacy of, 23, 25–6, 30, 35, 36, 42,
    51, 67, 99, 100
Felipe, Grandpa, 135
Felton, Carlos, 122, 138
Fernández, Joaquín, 143–4, 145

FitzRoy, Captain, 74
Foster, Maud, 85
Fotheringham, Alex, 129, 130
Fotheringham, Carina, 129, 136
Fotheringham, Ignatius 'Ignacio', 129
Fotheringham, Tomás, 128, 129
Fraser, David, 84, 115
Fraser, 'Dot' or 'Dottie', see David
    Fraser
Frazer family, 68–9, 106
Froebel, Friedrich, 65
Fueyo, Nohry, 154–5
Fullerton, Arlene, 27
Fullerton, William, 27

Galtieri, General Leopoldo, 17–18
Ganadera Colonel, 16
Gardiner, Allen, 41, 126, 127, 161
General Belgrano, 51, 128–9
Gilbert and Sullivan, 141
Gillies, Eva, 129
Gilmore, Mary, 141
Giuvetich, Nene, 114
Gónzalez, José, 43
Gónzalez, Maggie (née Goring), 43
Goodall, Clarita, 134
Goodall, John, 134
Goodall, Natalie (née Prosser), 135
Goodall, Tommy 'Thomas', 130, 133,
    134–5
Goose Green Stores, 26
Goring, George, 17, 18–19, 43, 128,
    134
Goring, Jeremy, 7, 9, 21, 22, 45, 47,
    57, 58, 61, 69–70, 92, 98, 100,
    105, 109, 113, 115, 117, 133, 138,
    141, 146, 157
Goring, Rosemary J. (née Blake)
    childhood in Patagonia 12, 13–14,
    15, 46, 57, 63, 64, 69, 88, 92–5,

98–9, 103, 104–14, 117–18,
    138–9, 141, 149–50, 159
San Julián, 14, 33, 44, 45, 92
Buenos Aires, 14, 15, 46, 47, 48–9,
    50–1, 56–7, 88
family and the Second World War,
    47, 50, 68–9, 88–9, 94, 105–6,
    107, 109, 118
leaving Coronel and San Julián,
    13–14, 44, 103, 115, 149–50,
    159
return to England, 14–15
childhood in England, 15–16, 142
trip to Falkland Islands (1992),
    Port Stanley, 23, 24, 27, 28–31;
    Goose Green, 24–5; Sea Lion
    Island, 26–7; West Falkland,
    33–42
trip to Patagonia (1999),
    Buenos Aires, 45–51; Trelew,
    53–61; Comodoro, 63–71; San
    Julián, 91–101; Coronel
    (Estancia), 103–14; Río Gallegos,
    115–23; Tierra del Fuego,
    125–36; Killik Aike, 137–47
Grange School, Santiago, 15, 88, 107
Great Britain, SS, 27
'Grey Dawn' (Aloyz de Simonato,
    Camila Raquel), 66–7
Grundig factory, Ushuaia, 130
'Gwyl y Glaniad', 53

Hamilton, Captain John, 37–8
Harberton (farm), 130, 133, 134
Harding, Hugh, 164
Harps Farm, 34
Harrods, Buenos Aires, 49
Henin, Leopoldo, 100–1, 119, 154
Herford, Dorothea 'Dora', see
    Dorothea Blake

Herford, William Henry, 65, 76
Hernández, Nicanor, 92
Hill Cove (farm), 18, 22, 24, 29, 33, 34, 36, 76, 77, 120–1, 150–1, 164
Hoffmann, Eva (née Bideleux), 158
Holdich, Sir Thomas, 56
Holmested, Ernest, 33, 37, 41, 76, 162, 163, 164
Holmested Blake, 29
Hostería América, Ushuaia, 128
Hotel Miramar, San Julián, 82, 94
Hunt, Sir Rex 27

In Patagonia (Bruce Chatwin), 122

Jackechan, 54, 55
Jenkins, Aaron, 55
John Paul II, Pope, 140
Jones, Aneurin Erasmus, 155–6
Jones, Colonel 'H', 25
Jones, Lewis, 53
Jones, Rachel, 55

Kami, Lake, *see* Lago Fagnano
Keillor, Garrison, 157
Kennard, Naomi, *see* Naomi O'Byrne
Kennedy, Alec, 99
Kennedy, Edith, 99
Kennedy, Ethel, 99
Kennedy, Heather, 99
Keokén, Gallegos, 116, 117, 146
Kew Gardens 65
Killik Aike Norte (farm), 7, 17–18, 122, 137–41, 143, 158
Kirchner, Néstor, 153, 154
Kyle, Andrew, 84, 152

LADE, 31
Laet, J. de, 74
Lago Argentino, 144, 145

Lago Escondido, 130, 131
Lago Fagnano, 130, 131–2
Lambert, Daisy, 146
Lambert, Ronald, 146
Lamont, Donald, 151
Lapataia National Park, 18, 128
Lee, Robin, 21
Le Maire, Jacob, 74
Lofredo, Florita, 117
Luna, Hector, 151

Madres (Mothers of the Disappeared), 48
Magellan, Ferdinand, 73, 161
Malvina House, Port Stanley, 42
Mann, Agnes, 14, 44, 92, 118, 158, 159
Mann, Alec, 91–2, 109, 117
Mann, Cath, 7, 44, 45, 91–101, 103–4, 113, 114, 115, 116, 152, 154
Mann, Dorothy, 116, 117, 147
Mann, Duncan, 119, 153, 154
Mann, George, 117
Mann, Mary, *see* Mary Pickering
Mann, Matilda, 92, 118
Mann, Sandy, 91, 116, 117, 120
Mann, Tilly, 114
Mann, Willie 118
Mansilla, Lucio, 129
Maritime Museum, Ushuaia, 132–3
Massey-Ferguson Prize, 143
Mathews, Edward, 79
Matthews, Abraham, 55–6
McPhee, Madge, 41–2
Mestivier, Governor, 163
Millam, Reverend Peter, 22
Mothers of the Disappeared, *see* Madres
Mount Hudson, eruption of, 95–7, 115, 156, 162, 164

Mount Pleasant (airport), 23, 42, 46
Moy, Augustus, 155
Moyano, Carlos, 75, 161, 164
Moyano, Emilio, 156
Munro, Donald, 13, 77, 81, 152, 162
Museo del Fin del Mundo, Ushuaia, 135
Musters, George, 53–4, 55

Narborough, John, 74
National School, San Julián, 156
Nelson, Horatio, 76
Northlands, Buenos Aires, 65

'O God Our Help in Ages Past', 47
O'Byrne, Erroll, 119, 146, 147
O'Byrne, Naomi, 119, 146, 147
Ona Indians, 131, 132, 135
Onslow, Captain, 163
'Oración Postuma' (Pablo Rodriguez), 128–9

Palermo Park, Buenos Aires, 50–1
Paloma, La (Sebastian Yradier) 142
Parachute Regiment, 118
Paradise Mislaid: In Search of the Australian Tribe of Paraguay (Anne Whitehead), 141
Parque Retiro, Buenos Aires, 47
Patagonia, flora and fauna of, 55, 60, 63, 75, 79, 99, 104, 105–6, 128, 131, 133, 138, 143, 144
'Patagonia' (Rosemary Goring), 12
Patagonian Harvest (Mary Trehearne), 7
Patagonian Missionary Society, see South American Missionary Society
'Patagonian Shadows' (Camila Raquel Aloyz de Simonato), 70
Patterson, Bob, 68–9
Patterson, Robert, 81

Peaks, The (farm), 29, 150, 164
Pearce, Bessie, 44, 45, 91–2, 96, 103, 118, 158, 159
Perito Moreno National Park, 143–5
Perón, Juan, 47, 49
Philco factory, Ushuaia, 130
Phoenix Hotel, Buenos Aires, 48–9, 146
Pickering, Adrian, 119
Pickering, Derick, 146
Pickering, Lidia, 7, 44, 45, 91–2, 94–6, 98, 99–100, 104–5, 106, 109, 111, 113, 114, 115, 116, 118, 149, 151, 153
Pickering, Lionel, 92, 96, 105, 107, 117, 118, 119, 162
Pickering, Mary (née Mann), 44, 45, 91–2, 104, 105, 107, 114, 116, 117, 118, 119, 147, 153, 154
Pickering, Tom, 92, 104, 113, 117, 118
Pigafetta, Antonio, 73
Pilgrim Fathers, 54
Pilkington, John, 7, 56, 57–8, 97, 116, 120, 122, 127
Pioneering Pig, The (Norman Blake), 29
Plas y Coed, Gaimán, 59
Ponce, Daniel, 115
Port Howard (farm), 24, 33–4, 36, 79, 121
Prensa, La, 49
Prosser, Natalie, see Natalie Goodall
Puerto Williams, 135

Radio Nacional Chile, 139
RAF Brize Norton, 23, 42
Rees, Marta, 59
Repton School, 77
Residencia Rivadavia, Trelew, 57
Retiro Station, Buenos Aires, 47
Revolt of the Catalanas, 85

Reynard, Henry, 161
Roca, President, 130
Rodriguez brothers, 83
Rodriguez, Pablo, 128–9
Roedean School, 7, 15, 77, 86, 87
Royal Air Force, 89

St David's School, Trelew, 14, 58, 158
St David's Association, Trelew, 58
Saint-Exupéry, Antoine de, 49–50, 57
St Hilda's School, Buenos Aires, 15,
  88, 119, 146
San Julián, history of, 68, 73–5, 77–9,
  81–5, 93–4, 151–7, 161, 162
San Julián Centenary Book, see Centenario
  de Puerto San Julián, Tomos I y II
San Julián Sheep Farming Company, see
  Coronel
Sara (Estancia), 117
Schmiegelow, Deaconess Patti, 39
School of Architecture, Bristol, 142
Schouten, Willem, 74
Sedbergh School, 77
74 Days: An Islander's Diary of the
  Falklands Occupation (John Smith),
  7, 31
Sheffield, HMS, 27
Silesian Fathers, 132
Siracusa, 103, 104, 162
Smith, John, 7, 30–1, 36, 100, 139
Smith, Tony, 27–8
Somerset Light Infantry, 82
Songs of Praise, 151
Sony factory, Ushuaia, 130
South American Missionary Society,
  40, 41, 126, 130, 163
South Atlantic Medal Association, 51
Southern Mail: Night Flight (Vol de Nuit)
  (Antoine de Saint-Exupéry), 50
Spafford, Major Ronnie, 22, 35

Sparrow's, Somerset, 78
Special Air Service, 37, 39
Sports Week, West Falkland, 24, 34–6,
  38
Sportsman, San Julián, 94
Spraggon, Monsignor Daniel, 30
Stanley Airport, 24
Stanley Museum, 30–1
Steele, Roberta, 146
Stirling, Reverend Whait, 41, 126, 161
Story of Patagonia, A (John Locke Blake),
  157–9
Strong, Captain John, 37, 163
Sullivan, Jackie, 7
Swift's, San Julián, 98

Talía, San Julián, 95, 152
Tehuelche Indians, 55, 73, 74, 137
Touring Club Hotel, Trelew, 57–8, 158
Trehearne, Brian, 158
Trehearne, Mary, 7, 82, 84, 151,
  157–8
Trelew, history of, 53–6, 59–60
Turner, Ethel, 75
2 Parachute Battalion, 25

United Nations, 21–2, 164
Upland Goose Hotel, Port Stanley, 24,
  30
Uppingham School, 77
Uttermost Parts of the Earth (Lucas
  Bridges), 125

Vernet, Louis, 163
Vernham, Miss, 156–7
Viedma, Antonio de, 74, 161
Visit to the Ranquel Indians, A (Mansilla,
  Lucio V.), 129
Vol de Nuit, see Southern Mail: Night
  Flight

Waldron, James Lovegrove, 33–4, 162, 163

War Graves Commission, 40

Waterloo, Battle of, 129

Wedderburn, Edith, *see* Edith Blake

Wedderburn, Midge, 87

Wellington, Duke of, 129

Western Daily Press, 88

Whitehead, Anne, 140–1

Wigglesworth, Angela, 7

World's End Museum, *see* Museo del Fin del Mundo

Worsley, Millicent, *see* Millicent Blake

Worsley, Philip, 14

Worsley, Philip, 86

Worsley, Piers, 18, 19

Yahgan Indians, 40–1, 126, 127, 130, 133, 135

Yradier, Sebastian, 142

Yudalevich, Yehuda Israel, *see* Julio Aloyz